LET'S
DO
THIS!

TESTIMONIALS

FIONA

I was unfit, unhealthy and stuck in a rut after a recent divorce. But I found the courage to join one of Andy's masterclasses and things got very exciting, very quickly. After building momentum with a few small wins, I stepped up to do a big challenge that would feed into my positivity streams of movement, nutrition and connection. I agreed to do a Spartan obstacle race – one of the toughest races on the planet. And I didn't stop there. I kept building up my confidence and self-esteem and eventually reached my life goal. This is what can happen when you join Andy on a masterclass. I thought doing a Spartan obstacle race was a massive achievement for someone who could barely walk to the shops and back. But look what I've achieved in the past month – from zero to opening my dream business, a new pharmacy! Clear mind, clear plans – clearly nuts!!!

GARY

I was born with spina bifida and have been wheelchair-bound for most of my life. When I reached my 40s, I had a sense that there was more to be had from this life thing. So I found the motivation to take a masterclass and stumbled upon my vocation. I'm a software engineer for my day job, but I have always had a very keen interest in personal development. I've read dozens and dozens of books on the subject, but the one thing that changed the game for me was doing the masterclass with Andy. More than any other piece of personal development material I've ever come across, his masterclass helped me find the thing. The thing I was born to do, and that thing is coaching.

The course gave me the momentum, confidence and courage to sign up for an executive and life-coaching diploma, which I have successfully completed.

As someone born with a disability, I am a passionate believer in the ability of every single human to achieve their potential. My plan now is to coach other disabled people to see that the only real limits they have are those that they put on themselves.

I've also been promoted since the masterclass and been chosen from over 150 candidates to sit on a national committee to advise on how Ireland can implement the United Nations Charter on the Rights of the Disabled. I can say with utter and complete certainty that none of this would have been possible without doing the masterclass. This was the thing that changed the game for me.

I have now found the thing. The thing I was born to do. I believe that even more now. What's next? Who knows?

LET'S DO THIS!

How to use motivational psychology to change your habits for life

ANDY RAMAGE

aster

FOR MY MOTIVATORS: TARA, MOLLY AND RUBY

An Hachette UK Company
www.hachette.co.uk

First published in Great Britain in 2019 by Aster,
an imprint of Octopus Publishing Group Ltd
Carmelite House
50 Victoria Embankment
London EC4Y 0DZ
www.octopusbooks.co.uk

Distributed in the US by
Hachette Book Group
1290 Avenue of the Americas
4th and 5th Floors
New York, NY 10104

Distributed in Canada by
Canadian Manda Group
664 Annette St.
Toronto, Ontario, Canada M6S 2C8

ISBN 978-1-78325-328-9

A CIP catalogue record for this book is available from the British
Library.

Printed and bound in the UK

10 9 8 7 6 5 4 3 2 1

Consultant Publisher Kate Adams
Senior Editor Pollyanna Poulter
Art Director Juliette Norsworthy
Production Controller Lisa Pinnell
Copy Editor Caroline Taggart
Proofreader Rachel Cross
Indexer MFE Editorial
Designer Jeremy Tilston
Illustration Claire Huntley

CONTENTS

Preface

Most of what we know about motivation is misleading. It's not something you're born with, or that you need to get from other people. Motivation is a skill that you can learn and this book will show you how.

Have you ever started a diet and stopped? Or created the perfect exercise plan only to drop it days, weeks or a couple of months later? Perhaps you committed to a savings scheme, but blew it on a must-have gadget or dress. Or you promised to quit smoking or cut back on the booze, but a strange force overcame you and quickly made you break your vows. What about the New Year's resolutions that never make it past the first week of January?

Maybe you feel a bit broken. Maybe you think you weren't born with the motivation gene, while some other lucky ones were. Perhaps you feel different from all those willpower warriors who appear to have motivation on tap.

But, equally, you're confused because in the past you have found the motivation to climb the corporate ladder or raise a loving family or reach health goals, like running a marathon. But still, certain things that you would love to achieve somehow elude you and you struggle to find the motivation to stay on track, despite all your great intentions.

Here's the thing. I've just described almost everyone on the planet, including me. We have all been in the same willpowerless boat, we have all ditched our goals in the face of instant gratification or given up at the first hint of failure.

This is not because we're broken. It's because we're human beings.

For years I struggled with motivation. I eventually assumed I was a lost cause and gave up. By my mid-30s I was overweight, unfit, unhappy and unmotivated. But something happened that was to transform my life and I set out on a quest for the key to unlock lasting motivation. And I found it.

This may come as a surprise, but right now you have all the motivation you'll ever need. It's just misdirected. This is why you achieve in one area of your life and look like a motivational disaster in others. The books, courses and thought leaders are selling a willpower dream you'll rarely reach. That's why this book is not about willpower: it's about learning the skills to master good old motivation.

Part 1 will present several secrets that will transform the way you view your motivation. Each secret will build on the next as you prepare for motivational mastery.

Then, in Part 2, before you choose your goal, you will review the six streams of positivity, which are the foundations of a fully motivated life. Using this knowledge, I will show you how to get tactical with your goals so you can leverage the feedback from your six streams scores to build the momentum you need to succeed. You will also discover that motivation is not about the goal; it's about owning and creating a plan. By taking extreme ownership of your plan, you take control of motivation.

In Part 3, I will share my 28-day motivational masterclass that has helped thousands of people just like you to overcome their biggest challenges and achieve their goals. The masterclass is the result of ten years of examining the best scientific research and techniques to create a motivational system that works for real people like you and me.

And the most exciting part? Your plan will last a lifetime. To achieve your next goal you simply drop it into your existing motivational plan. You then repeat the process to achieve the next goal, and the next...

PART 1

Let's Do the Prep

Chapter 1
How a Marshmallow Misled Us

In the 1960s, a groundbreaking psychologist called Walter Mischel set up a study that was to change the face of motivation. But the results have led the majority of us astray. Because almost everything we know about motivation is wrong.

Imagine you're four years old. With a bowl-cut and flares, you arrive at preschool to an air of excitement. Your teacher introduces Walter, the dad of a classmate, who explains he is conducting a fun experiment that involves marshmallows. Keep in mind that the original study took place at Stanford University's illustrious Bing preschool in California, so the scientist dads were basically rock stars. Had David Beckham popped in to show the kids keepy-uppies they would have yelled, "Bore off, Becks, show us the science."

Now imagine one by one you are ushered into a space the researchers dubbed the "surprise room", because they never knew what they would see through the observation glass. Inside, Walter, the super-cool dad, places a tempting marshmallow on the table in front of you. Before he leaves the room, he offers a trade:

"If you don't eat the marshmallow while I'm gone, you can have another tasty marshmallow when I return. But if you eat this one while I'm away, you don't get a second marshmallow."

Can you imagine the impossibility of this challenge? I would have had the marshmallow in my mouth before Walter made his offer. I know it's rude to snatch, but…marshmallows, man.

What happened next was just harsh. Rather than having a quick two-minute chat and returning, Walter waited outside for up to 15 minutes.

A few of the children wiggled, others sang, many jumped up and down or looked away, all in a desperate bid to avoid temptation. Eventually most of the preschoolers crumbled and scoffed the marshmallow. The conclusion from the initial research suggested that children who utilized diversion tactics were able to resist the marshmallow the longest. As a stand-alone piece of research, the discovery that distraction techniques were most effective proved a worthwhile experiment. So the marshmallows were packed away (eaten) and the test forgotten. That was until a chance conversation was to change the way we view motivation.

The marshmallow falls from the tree

Several years after the original marshmallows test, enlightenment struck when Mischel and his daughter, now a teenager, discussed her naughty classmates, many of whom had taken part in the original study.

Just like at most schools, the same kids always seemed to be in trouble, while others would behave themselves, do their homework and excel. Suddenly, the marshmallow fell from the tree. Mischel wondered if the behaviour of the teenagers had any correlation to the findings from the marshmallow study?

So, Mischel and his crack team (his daughter) rounded up all the participants from the original experiment. By fluke, the wait outside had only been meant to uncover the children's delaying tactics. But the length of time they resisted had also been recorded. Mischel was able to compare the children's delay times with how their life had progressed since the study. It was the disregarded delay times that would fundamentally change the way we now view self-control.

The four-year-olds who held out for the full 15 minutes would, as teenagers, score an average of 210 points higher on their SAT tests than those who caved and hoovered up the marshmallow after less than 30 seconds.

The American SAT test is a big deal – it's a bit like British A-levels. So this was a major discovery. These superpower delayers were also rated as more popular among their classmates and teachers.

Mischel did not stop there: he kept track of these teenagers into adulthood and the results grew even more interesting. As he enthused in his cult book *The Marshmallow Test*, the delayers were "less distractible when trying to concentrate; were more intelligent, self-reliant, and confident; and trusted their own judgment." What's more, "when motivated they were more able to pursue their goals."

In adulthood, the children who delayed the longest went on to earn higher salaries than the others and were less prone to addictions. They were considered more successful and were better

IN ADULTHOOD, THE CHILDREN WHO DELAYED THE LONGEST WENT ON TO EARN HIGHER SALARIES AND WERE LESS PRONE TO ADDICTIONS

at reaching long-term goals. They also had a healthier BMI (body mass index), were more resilient and better able to maintain close relationships.

Popular culture embraced the findings as a signpost toward achievement. "Don't eat the marshmallows" t-shirts were printed. *Sesame Street*'s Cookie Monster even tried to resist marshmallows in a noble attempt to inspire children to do the same. If that big blue shaggy puppet could do it, there was hope for us all, right?

The scientific community was enthralled by the findings. It was so rare for something measured in childhood to potentially predict outcomes into adulthood. Although scientists acknowledged there might be a genetic component, it seemed that having the willpower to delay gratification was the pathway to happiness and success.

Another brilliant scientist, the social psychologist Roy Baumeister, whom we shall see more of in chapter 3, picked up the willpower baton and concluded: "Self-regulation failure is the major social pathology of our time."

Not only was it a huge benefit to have the power to delay, but those unfortunates who lacked self-control were also statistically more likely to commit crimes, suffer from depression, have eating disorders, be in abusive relationships and worse.

In summary, if you were lucky enough to find the motivation to delay gratification as a four-year-old, you were able to study longer, eat more healthily, exercise more, earn more cash and, to top it off, be happier. These findings were inspiring and it was exciting to believe that mastering control could lead to so many motivational benefits. Then I demolished a whole pack of cookies and the delay theory came crashing down.

Mischel's study was fantastic news for the few four-year-olds for whom delaying comes naturally. But what about the rest of us?

What if you have wobbly willpower?

Like Mary, who's determined to save for a deposit on a house, but keeps blowing her money on yet another bargain?

Or Sally, who's trying to shape up, but can't resist those tempting leftover French fries on her daughter's plate?

Or Lenny the box-set binger, who promises to get more sleep, only to start just one more *Game of Thrones* at 1am?

Or Mark, who is disillusioned with his job, but can't find the mojo to do something about it?

Or my dad, who, after his hundredth "last" Indian takeaway, is absolutely, definitely starting his diet?

Or the gym members who never show up? The folks who have kitchens packed with unused gadgets or garages full of expensive racing bikes?

What about us?

We were forgotten.

Until now.

HOW WE ARE SETTING OURSELVES UP TO FAIL:

- WE RELY ON WILLPOWER
- OUR WILLPOWER WOBBLES
- WE FAIL
- WE BEAT OURSELVES UP
- WE GIVE UP

Chapter 2
From Miserable to Motivated – My Story

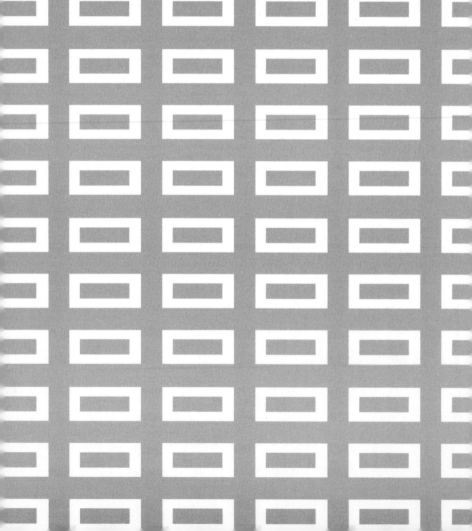

Just a few years ago I could barely motivate myself to get out of bed. I was unfit, dreadfully unhealthy, unmotivated and unhappy. I was a typical meat-eating, salad-dodging City type who drank too much.

My job had left me stressed out, maxed out and my relationships were strained across the board. Luckily my wife Tara was always supportive, but I was in danger of becoming a bore who was always too tired to enjoy our time together. My kids had stopped asking me to play with them because they knew the answer. And my colleagues had started to notice my inconsistent performance. I felt as though I had zero free time as I chased the conventional dream of earning enough money to finally reach that place where happiness apparently lives. To top it all off, I had just discovered I had heart disease, which scared the life out of me. How had I let this happen? I had once been such a healthy, fun-loving, happy-go-lucky, life-and-soul type of character. Yet here I was. Broken.

It was at this point that I knew something had to change. But I didn't know where to begin. And it wasn't that I totally lacked motivation. I was great at getting started – just awful at the follow through.

Then I discovered a secret that was to change the course of my life.

How turning water into beer created a small miracle

Three weeks into yet another attempt to take a break from the booze, fired up by my rational choice to give up alcohol, I walked into the lions' den (the bar). As I joined the scrum of thirsty punters and waited my turn to order a water, a question cut through the beer-soaked air:

"What would you like to drink?"

I paused and, with confidence, said, "I'll have a pint of beer, please." *What!* How did that happen? Where did my water go?

Confused and intrigued by my biblical ability to turn water into beer, I cursed my lack of motivation. Once again I'd failed.

But I didn't give up completely. I was desperate to know more. So I set out on a quest to solve a motivational riddle whose answer has eluded us for too long: how could someone like me, who was hopeless at delaying gratification, find the consistent motivation to achieve my goals and dreams?

Having worked myself to the bone to achieve the career, the beautiful family and a house full of gadgets gathering dust, I couldn't help thinking, is this it? I'd been driven by a conventional wisdom that suggested that, when I had these status symbols, eternal bliss would be mine. You can imagine my disappointment when I discovered, not for the first time, that conventional wisdom was wrong.

I looked around at the people who were more "successful" than me and was horrified. They were exhausted from long commutes, late nights and lack of family time. All because they were chasing the same false dream. What was the point? I didn't aspire to this. Bodies, minds, families all broken on a quest for conventional success.

I knew I couldn't be the only one who wanted more from life.

I started to ask new questions: What if my problem wasn't a lack of motivation? What if I had all the motivation I needed, but didn't know how to use it? And what if almost everyone else also had this motivation thing wrong?

Excited, I set out to crack the motivation code so there would be no need for a never-ending list of New Year's resolutions because I would actually, for the first time ever, achieve my goals. I'd keep the promises I made to myself and create a life that made me genuinely happy.

Full of inspiration, I set out on my greatest adventure. No, not going to Disneyland or climbing Kilimanjaro. I set out to understand everything I could about motivation and how to make behavioural changes stick. This mission to solve the motivation puzzle took me around the world from Dubai to LA to the Maldives and, finally, to the not-exactly-glittering London suburb of Croydon. I trained with the best coaches, motivational gurus and thought leaders, such as the co-founder of neuro-linguistic programming, John Grinder; world free-diving champion Sara Campbell; one of the world's fittest men over 50, Rich Roll; and addiction expert Dr Gabor Maté, to name a few.

I even went back to university – twice! – to finish an Open University degree and then to complete a master's degree in positive psychology and coaching psychology. Over the last ten years, I have devoured thousands of clinical studies and textbooks searching for the code to unlock unlimited motivation.

After years of investigating, I found what I was looking for: **motivation is a skill that anyone can learn.** My mission in this book is to share my motivation masterclass with you.

Imagine, by the end of this book you will own a motivational plan that will allow you to consistently smash your goals. Maybe you want to get fit, start a new business, learn a language, find more time, quit smoking, drink less or travel more? This is your moment to make it happen. So follow me, and let's do this.

Find your motivation, change your life

Armed with newfound knowledge, a big smile and a suntan, I returned from my quest full of motivation to set up a new broking business. Only this time things were going to be different. I was going to meditate, exercise and eat salad and stuff.

With a motivational fast pass swinging from my neck, I was ready to test the system and take down the big one. The ultimate social challenge. A challenge so gigantic that I had failed hundreds of times before. I quit alcohol.

There was no problem. I was a middle-lane drinker who drank moderately, sometimes averagely and occasionally heavily – like almost everyone else I knew. But I was guilty of the worst trade in the history of trades: exchanging a Friday night's drinking for a hungover weekend. When I was younger, losing the best two days of the week to a hangover didn't matter as much. But once I had kids, the thought of another weekend wasted due to self-inflicted lethargy was killing me. Literally. I wanted to be a fun-time dad, not a tired-can't-be-arsed-I-feel-sick dad. And I had big plans for my life, but I couldn't find the time, energy or motivation to do anything about them.

The worst part was the inconsistency that alcohol created. I would set out on the road to getting fit and healthy, but a couple of beers at the end of the day would derail my plans. Healthy food options kept turning into stodge and gym sessions morphed into Netflix. And my performance at work was totally inconsistent. I could kick ass like a superhero for a few days and then do almost nothing when the morning-after hangxiety kicked in.

I was also inconsistent in my relationships. My wife Tara summed it up perfectly: "Some days you were – well, like you, full of energy – while others you looked withdrawn, tired and not quite right." It's amazing how tiredness, stress and hangovers can combine to suck the happiness out of life. Instead of having fun I was grumpy, which was not me.

When I was 16 years old and about to embark on my career as a professional footballer, my dad passed on some advice that stuck with me. He said, "Never be the drunk at the end of the bar who says, 'I could have made it, if it weren't for…'" Suddenly, in my mid-30s, I was dangerously close to becoming that guy. Ultimately alcohol was having a negative impact on the most important thing in my life, my family. So something had to change.

I knew that alcohol, of all my motivational failures, was the one that was holding me back the most. If the motivational masterclass I had created was to work for everyone, then it had to stand up to the behemoth behavioural change that is taking a break from the booze.

To my friends, wife and colleagues, this particular challenge appeared crazy. Why would anyone stop drinking alcohol unless they were a grizzly alcoholic nursing a can of Special Brew on a park bench?

I have to admit the thought of taking a long-term break from alcohol scared the pants off me. At this stage in my life booze played a big role. It was how I celebrated, commiserated, de-stressed and socialized. Entertaining (corporate codeword for drinking) was a massive part of my job as a commodities broker. And I was great at it. I could polish off a bottle of vino collapso for lunch, close a few deals and be back out for a beer before sundown. But living this way had made my life more about stress and survival than enjoyment.

I often fantasized about finding the motivation to take a break from the booze, and how this might be a gateway to the life I always wanted.

Spoiler alert. It was.

Armed with my motivation masterclass, I took a break from the booze for the 237th time – and this time I actually stuck to it. Like a ginger alcohol-free superhero, I dodged the social pressure and made it to 28 days alcohol-free.

Cue fireworks.

On the face of it, you wouldn't think a month off the booze would furnish such a revelation but, wow, it did. My 28th day was a Saturday and I woke that morning having slept like a baby. My body felt refreshed, my eyes were bright and the sun was shining. My wife was in love with me and I was in love with her. Even the kids were on top form and I felt great, really great. In that moment of bliss, I knew I was on to something.

With this success under my belt, my motivational skills went to the next level. From 28 clear-headed days, I eventually climbed the one-year-no-beer mountain. As I raised my alcohol-free flag, I knew this was no longer about the booze. I had cracked the long-term motivational code.

And what happened next was even more exciting.

The motivational snowball

Full of confidence in the motivational masterclass, I started to take on other challenges. The next big one for me was my diet. At this point, I weighed in at 15.3 stone. That's 97kg (214lb). My body fat was over 35 per cent, when doctors say that a healthy man of my age should have 8–19 per cent. I looked more pregnant than a pig expecting quintuplets. Or as my mate Colm pointed out, "You're the image of Ricky Hatton [the former world champion boxer] going through his fat stage."

David Attenborough would have described me like this: "Here we have a midlife ginger *Homo sapiens*. He eats meat and dodges vegetables." My diet was almost entirely beige in colour. I would eat everything apart from the green stuff.

Fast-forward a few months and, after lots of research into the best diet for me, I became one of those super-trendy vegans and the weight started to fall off.

How? Simple: I just used my motivational plan to eat differently. This was a lifestyle, not a quick fix. And the best part – I felt great. Really great. Eating a whole rainbow of vegetables filled me with energy and those afternoon slumps evaporated.

There's more. For years I had battled with rosacea, which is a skin condition that creates red blotches and pimples across your nose and cheeks. So attractive. The great irony was that rosacea is associated with the classic whisky-drinker's red nose. I had already stopped drinking, so it was bloody annoying to look as though I was still smashing back the shots. I hoped that quitting alcohol would cure it, but it hadn't. I was gutted. My GP informed me that rosacea was a chronic condition. I asked if there was anything I could do. He explained that rosacea could be caused by sunlight, spicy food, exercise, sugar, wheat... Translation: I don't have a clue – it could be anything. He gave me some pills that I would have to take for the rest of my life and sent me on my way.

But the rosacea kept coming back. The less I was drinking, the more it looked as if I was drinking. Then something almost magical happened. I changed my diet and the rosacea vanished.

The chronic, lifelong, forever-pill-taking, whisky-drinking, blotchy, pimpled skin cleared up.

I still don't know the exact food group that was causing it – burgers? cookies? – but I do know for a fact that finding the motivation to try a plant-based diet cured a so-called chronic condition. I find it endlessly frustrating that many medical professionals appear to have lost all faith in our society's ability to make lasting behavioural change. It's as though they assume that no one is capable of finding the motivation to do anything transformative to combat disease, so they just prescribe us pills, forever, and move on to the next patient.

But here's the thing. The science is almost overwhelming that diet alone can cure many of our Western lifestyle diseases. All you need is the motivation to transform the way you eat and, in doing so, transform your health. This was the first time my motivational actions had defied the medical profession, but it wasn't the last, as you will find out later. As my skin started to glow thanks to my new healthy-eating regime, I was tempted to grow a trendy beard to celebrate. I had tried a million diets in the past, but nothing had ever lasted more than a few weeks. Nothing had ever felt so good. And the great news is that a new wave of doctors like Alan Desmond, whom you will meet on day 23 of the masterclass, are showing the masses how to transform their diets and health.

Applying the same motivational masterclass had allowed me to transform my relationship with alcohol and now the way I ate – permanently. Time is the true test of the motivational process and six years later I am still alcohol-free and eating mostly plants.

TIME IS THE TRUE TEST OF THE MOTIVATIONAL PROCESS

The upward spiral of motivation

A teacher once told me that learning a new language is like creating an extra filter in your ear. You learn a third language quicker because more information gets through. The skill of motivation is the same. Each time you apply the plan to one area of your life, the next challenge becomes a little easier. In my example, learning the skills to take a break from alcohol made it easier to transform my diet. With alcohol and my diet under control, starting an exercise routine was easier again. And so on.

Next on my motivational hit list was fitness. Twenty years earlier I'd been a professional footballer, so you'd think I'd have the exercise thing covered. But no. My gym routine involved sitting in the steam room, then sitting in the jacuzzi. In other words, my fitness had flat-lined.

As I've said, I was carrying a fair bit of extra timber and lugging this weight around the dance floor of life was tough. But with the momentum I had from my alcohol-free adventure and a plant-based diet, I found the extra motivation to reignite my love for exercise.

Buried under the 35 per cent body fat was a 10 per cent slender athlete screaming to get out. All I had to do was apply my motivation masterclass and release the lean beast.

Motivation is here to stay

Before I mastered motivation, when I felt tired and lethargic most of the time, I clearly remember thinking, "I guess this is just how you're meant to feel when you hit middle age." What a load of rubbish. Here I was a few months later and I had more energy than when I was in my 20s. I looked and felt ten years younger.

Consistently eating well, exercising and not drinking created an upward spiral of health. My before and after photos looked like two different people. My family could not get over the change in my appearance: not only had I lost weight, but my eyes were bright again, my confidence had returned and I was buzzing.

With the motivation to start – and stick to – my fitness plan, I stripped my body fat down to a healthy 10 per cent and lost three stone in three months. That's 19kg (42lb)! As much as a full sack of potatoes! Or 34 basketballs! What's more, it didn't even feel like a struggle. In fact, I loved it. And the most astounding part is that all these healthy motivational changes combined to shock my cardiologist.

Why have we lost faith in our ability to make dramatic change?

"Astounding, quite astounding." Within two minutes of our meeting, this was the sixth (and seventh!) time my cardiologist Dr Gupta had repeated the word "astounding".

Only a couple of years earlier our conversation had been very different. At the age of 35 I was showing the early signs of heart disease. Following my dad's triple bypass, my two brothers and I had a full medical. I was the only one who scored badly. A calcium test that checks for furring of the arteries revealed that mine were filling up with life-threatening plaque. My heart sank.

For most of my life I'd been the fittest guy in the room. From the age of ten I was signed with a professional football club. My dreams came true at 16 and I went pro, spending the next 8 years living the dream only to have my career cut short due to injury. Without the boundaries of matches and training I was let loose. For the next few years I partied hard and travelled the world with my now wife. Then I hit the City of London to make my fortune. The suntan faded, along with my exercise routines.

Twelve hours a day at the desk, punctuated with boozy lunches and late nights, took their toll. Over the next decade I built a successful business, but there were sacrifices. My health was one of them. "It's part of the job," I would tell my wife when I arrived home late, again. Drunk, again. My daughters were getting used to me leaving and returning while they slept. Was I exceptional? Absolutely not. Take a look around. This is too often the norm.

On the way to the surgery for my first visit to Dr Gupta, I noticed a kebab shop. I walked past. Then backed up. I thought, depending on how this meeting goes, this might be the last doner kebab I can ever eat. "Large doner please, extra chilli sauce!"

Dr Gupta got straight to the point. "Andy, you have heart disease." I was not shocked. I'd been expecting it.

How sad. I'd gambled away my health for a career and cash.

If you change nothing, nothing changes

A year later I was back with Dr Gupta for a routine check-up. I was embarrassed that nothing had changed since we last met. I consoled myself with the thought that the cholesterol tablets were making up for my lack of ability to make proactive change. I got the impression this was standard. A patient assumes they are genetically predisposed to heart disease, they take pills and get on with life. Their unhealthy lifestyle remains as unhealthy as ever.

But something was different. I was close to starting my quest to find the truth about motivation and I was wrestling with the idea that if I could master my motivation I would use it to stop drinking first. I was still caught up with this thought when I met with Dr Gupta that second time. When I entered the room, I instantly felt a sense of sadness that I'd changed so little. It felt like my life was literally on the line, and I'd done precisely nothing about it. I was desperate to display some glimmer of motivational control. "Just so you know, Dr Gupta, I am going to give up alcohol. See you next year."

He smiled like someone who has heard it all before. His eyes said, people like you rarely change. I don't blame him. Our world is littered with unfulfilled resolutions, failed intentions and diets that start tomorrow. Even though I knew he did not believe me, it felt good to say it out loud, because I felt a surge of empowerment.

Almost exactly one year after Dr Gupta's seen-it-all smile, I was back. Only this time I was excited. Twelve months into my motivational adventure, I felt amazing. Full of vitality. I bounced into his office looking like a new person.

Now it was time to see if the test results matched how I felt.

"Astounding," Dr Gupta said. "Your resting heart rate has plummeted from 68 to 44, cholesterol is fantastic, your blood pressure is lower, you're 19kg (42lb) lighter and you look great. But what's truly phenomenal is that you appear to have slowed the signs of heart disease. In fact we were so interested in your results that we took a closer look. You've reversed it."

When I finally released the good doctor from my embrace, we both smiled. This time his eyes were full of admiration. I had done what most people consider impossible in our modern society. I had fundamentally improved my lifestyle to such an extent that my diseased arteries were healing.

I had just unleashed a motivation snowball that led to massive positive change.

I HAD DONE WHAT MOST PEOPLE CONSIDER IMPOSSIBLE IN OUR MODERN SOCIETY

Chapter 3
When Willpower Doesn't Work

As you do on a Saturday morning, I decided to recreate the marshmallow experiment with my daughters Molly and Ruby, who were aged twelve and nine at the time. This was less clinical and more comical than Walter's original research, but it was a peep into the mind of a child genius. I brought both girls into the kitchen, presented a marshmallow and laid out the deal: "If you don't eat it before I return, you can have two."

As I listened at the door, seconds later the girls were giggling so much they could barely breathe.

I flung the door open to the sight of zero marshmallows. My heart sank. That was it. They were doomed, I tell thee, doomed! Destined for poor grades, obesity, unhappiness and probably criminal records too. I wanted to cry.

Then came the bombshell.

I asked why they had crumbled so quickly and in a brilliant piece of emotional intelligence, Ruby responded, "I only wanted one, so why wait?"

Phew, there's hope for us all.

Ruby's clever retort revealed the problem with research like the marshmallow study. There is an assumption that the conclusions apply to everyone, but the results don't look at individual cases. Lots of people who were awful at delaying could have ended up super-happy and successful, but the average of all the participants told a slightly misleading story. And perhaps having the mental agility like Ruby to make something up on the spot and sound convincing might be ten times more valuable in the real world than cast-iron willpower or the ability to delay gratification.

You see, Walter Mischel's research was both groundbreaking and in many ways misleading. If you're like me, Ruby and the majority of the planet who are hopeless at delaying gratification, then I have great news. Forget trying to find willpower to fulfil your motivational dreams, because it doesn't work. The secret I will show you is that motivation is a skill that anyone can learn.

Let's Not Do This

For years I'd set up my life goals like one of Mischel's marshmallow experiments. My mission was normally to use willpower to resist the marshmallow of not doing the task. When I first set myself the goal of studying, I had to use willpower to force myself to resist the marshmallow of not studying. When I got back into exercise, a coach told me to swim, which I could not stand, so I had to apply willpower to resist the marshmallow of not swimming.

I didn't have the willpower to delay gratification for long, so eventually I would eat the not-swimming marshmallow and not do the task I had set for myself. My goals would slip through my fingers. I began to believe that I was broken and everyone else was a motivational machine. Then I looked around and discovered that almost everyone I knew was in the same willpowerless boat.

Are we mad?

If Einstein was right when he said, "The definition of madness is doing the same thing over and over and expecting a different result", then we're all mad, and willpower is responsible. How many times have you tried to quit coffee, stop checking your phone in front of the kids or leave the office on time, only to give up a few weeks, days, minutes later?

This was the story of my life. I'd grumbled, "Never again" a thousand times, and continually promised I'd change, only to go back to my old ways within days.

Let me ask – how's the willpower dream going for you? Not very well, I would guess. But don't worry. You, me and the rest of the planet all seem to have the willpower of a gnat.

A whopping 80 per cent of us are struggling to reach the recommended amount of monthly exercise, according to a UK study by the University of Bristol. We can't seem to lose weight to literally save our lives, with over 62 per cent of the UK population now considered dangerously overweight or obese. One in two of us are unhappy in our jobs and would like to change careers, according to recent research from the London School of Business and Finance.

I can't bring myself to continue with more gloomy stats, so I'll get to the point: using willpower alone is failing us on an epic scale.

When I first read the famous marshmallow study, I accepted the results as fact. I was convinced that if I had taken this test as a child I would have crumbled within seconds. Like any true Brit, I only had to get a sniff of a digestive biscuit near a nice cup of tea and the whole packet was dunked. I was a willpower failure and I knew it. But equally, I'd found the motivation to succeed as a professional footballer, to create a great business and also nurture a loving family. I was confused.

It was time to tuck-dive back into science.

THE GYM SESSION AFTER
WORK FEELS LIKE A GREAT
IDEA IN THE MORNING

How resisting chocolate messes with your brain

Once again a genius researcher wheeled out a sugary torture device to investigate willpower and motivation. Roy Baumeister of Florida State University seated his participants in front of warm cookies, chocolate bars and a seriously unappealing bowl of raw radishes. Once again the participants had to wait around while the researchers took note of their misery behind two-way glass.

One group of students were told they could eat the cookies, while another group were told they could only eat the radishes. The radish crew employed various tactics to resist, including smelling the cookies up close or looking away.

But unlike Mischel's marshmallow test, the radishes and cookies were a warm-up before the real action.

After the students had waited long enough, they were summoned into another room and presented with a puzzle, but there was a twist: the puzzle was impossible to solve. The impossible puzzle is a standard way to test for perseverance. Research continually demonstrates that those who persist the longest on a task that is unsolvable will keep working longer and harder on tasks that can be completed. Baumeister and his team wanted to know how long it took the students to quit working on the puzzle. The results were to expose willpower's major flaw.

The control group, who were not put in front of any food and simply had to take the test, lasted an average of 20 minutes before giving up on the puzzle.

Those who were allowed to eat the cookies also lasted 20 minutes.

But the participants who had to sit in front of the cookies but could only eat the radishes lasted just eight dismal minutes. Eight! That's not even half as long as the others.

The difference between the two groups was astounding. Baumeister concluded that willpower "seemed to be like a muscle that could be fatigued through use". In other words, the more willpower you exert, the quicker it runs out. Applying self-control not to eat the cookies had drained the students' willpower reserves, so they had less staying power on the impossible puzzle task.

This explains why tasks that run on willpower get harder as the day progresses. The gym session after work feels like a great idea in the morning, but when 6pm strikes you're tired, so you give yourself the night off.

And the willpower problem doesn't end there. We also use willpower to regulate our emotions. When our tanks are low, we are quicker to lose our temper. The maxed-out parent snaps at the kids who won't eat their dinner. The stressed-out partner gets home from work and flips because the bins haven't been put out (sorry, Tara).

Baumeister exposed the Achilles heel of willpower – trying to make lasting change on willpower alone will always end in disaster

WILLPOWER...

- IS ALL ABOUT SELF-CONTROL
- TAKES AWAY – STOP THIS, DON'T DO THAT
- RUNS OUT
- DRAINS YOUR ENERGY
- ZAPS CONFIDENCE

because it runs out. Admittedly, there are a lucky few who appear to be blessed with a significant stash of the stuff, like the super-delaying children, but most of the planet is like you and me.

I then asked the question: if willpower doesn't work, surely there has to be another way? In wrestling with this problem I unlocked another motivational truth. **Lasting motivation is not found by resisting marshmallows – it begins when you eat them!**

MOTIVATION...

- ## GIVES YOU A REAL REASON TO MAKE A CHANGE

- ## FOCUSES ON WHAT YOU CAN GAIN

- ## GROWS

- ## SNOWBALLS YOUR ENERGY

- ## BUILDS CONFIDENCE

Chapter 4
Eat the Marshmallows

Imagine you have two brains. The first is the primitive, reptilian and emotional brain that was once a fish. This part of your brain is an evolutionary miracle. It has fought, bitten, clawed and procreated its way through the ages of ages from the ocean to the savannah. Now it executes evolution's plan. Its interests include moving away from pain toward pleasure, saving energy and getting your genes into the next generation.

The second brain is the human, rational one that appeared on the scene 70,000 years ago during what is known as the cognitive revolution. This was the moment we became distinct from all the other animals, because we developed a new section of brain called the prefrontal cortex. This new "human" brain gave us the gift of foresight and with it the ability to worry endlessly about things that might never happen. This brain is "you" the human who is reading these words. The human brain takes a balanced approach to life and fully supports your motivational goals.

On the primitive brain's to-do list are tasks linked to evolutionary survival. It completes these life-prolonging errands on emotions and gut feel. It's often paranoid, prone to overreaction, expects the worst, makes choices based on black and white emotional thinking and is generally irrational. Sound familiar?

The human brain's to-do list is all about self-fulfilment. Tasks might include goals you want to achieve combined with a search for meaning. The human brain likes to use rational decision-making, consulting the evidence before reacting. It also has the ability to see the bigger picture and keep things in context while making logical choices. Hopefully that sounds familiar too.

Funnily enough, both brains are excellent at their jobs. The primitive brain is the best in the business at survival and the human brain is great at the rational. But they clash, big time. When the primitive brain throws a tantrum over a parking ticket, the human brain feels ashamed. Does this give you licence to shout at your boss and blame your reptilian, emotional, primitive brain? No. You have a responsibility to manage the primitive part of your brain. When you do, your world gets brighter.

While I'm on a roll, here's a secret to a good life: learn the skills to manage your primitive brain so it allows your human brain to achieve self-fulfilment, meaning and purpose.

Most of us make the schoolboy/girl error of assuming that you get to make every decision using this lovely shiny rational brain. Job done. Motivation is yours.

Here's the thing. When it comes to motivation, the primitive part of your brain always has the final say. This makes total sense because its job is survival. Finding food is more important than finding meaning. Evolution values survival over purpose, so the primitive brain is much stronger than the human one. And very often the primitive brain does not care for your "great" human ideas. If your primitive brain decides it wants a marshmallow, your human brain can't stop it. This is why salads turn into burgers, water into wine and gym sessions into Netflix marathons.

But here's the kicker, and a major insight that will transform your motivation – you can use your super-clever human brain to switch the metaphorical marshmallow in your mind. This sleight of hand gives you back control of motivation. You can use your rational human brain to decide which marshmallows your primitive brain sees. When you create the right healthy marshmallows in your mind, you don't have to use willpower to resist them. You can eat them. In doing so, you change the motivational game.

Let me explain

In Mischel's study the children had to resist a real marshmallow. The sugary treat is seriously tempting to the primitive brain because it's all about instant gratification. Your primitive brain wants it, right now. It doesn't care about you looking good in your swimsuit in six weeks. Survival depends on getting what you need in the present moment.

The only way to stop the primitive brain eating the marshmallow is to use willpower. But as we know, willpower is a short-term fix. The only difference between the exceptional super-delayers and most of us is that they are able to find deeper pockets of willpower – they can hold off the primitive brain for longer. But everyone's willpower eventually runs out. So trying to achieve your motivational goals on willpower alone will almost always end in a sugary mess. Unless you think outside the box.

Here's another key point – unless you take control, goals that require motivation produce metaphorical marshmallows you have to resist.

For example, imagine your goal is to get fit. You decide to start running, but you've not run in years and it feels like a massive slog. To find the motivation to get started you follow the traditional model and create lots of reasons why you "should" go for a run. Like...

- I want to get fit again
- My doctor says I need to exercise more
- I want to feel my best on holiday

So you plan to run the following day. The morning arrives, you have a quick conversation in your head about the merits of running today and guess what? You decide to sack it off. You'll start tomorrow.

How many times has a version of this happened to you?

What's happening, and you can imagine a similar scenario played out across all your motivational challenges, is that your primitive brain is seeing the wrong marshmallow. Remember, the primitive brain only cares about now.

If you don't have a motivational plan, like the one I will show you in the 28-day masterclass that is the focus of this book, the only thing your primitive brain sees is the I-can't-be-arsed-to-run marshmallow. From an evolutionary standpoint your primitive brain is trying to figure out why on earth you should use energy running when you can chill in front of the TV.

To complete step one of your goal – going for a run – you have to use willpower to stop your primitive brain from eating the I-can't-be-arsed-to-run marshmallow. But if your willpower is as weak as mine, your human brain gets overpowered. So the primitive brain eats the wrong (I-can't-be-arsed-to-run) marshmallow and you skip the run.

This was the story of my life, whatever goal I set. I could get started, but after a few days I would run out of willpower and stop doing the thing I wanted to do. It was driving me nuts.

But then I figured it out. What if I could use my human rational brain to focus on healthy metaphorical marshmallows that would satisfy my primitive brain? If I did that, I would no longer need willpower because both my human and primitive brains would want the same thing.

Changing marshmallows is not as easy as pointing at the window and yelling, "Look at the birdie" while doing a quick switch-a-roo. Changing your marshmallows takes a bit of mental elbow grease and time, but the rewards are gigantic. And this is not a one-off, white-board, red-pen, brainstorming moment. You might need to overwrite years of psychological programming. During week 3 of the motivational masterclass, I will show you exactly how to do just that.

Just What Is an I-Can't-Be-Arsed Marshmallow?

The I-can't-be-arsed marshmallow appears whenever your untrained, primitive brain thinks a task will use too much precious, life-saving energy. The primitive brain does not see the point in swimming or studying because they both require lots of energy. This produces the I-can't-be-arsed marshmallow, which you have to resist with willpower, but as you know willpower runs out. The trick, therefore, that I will show you over the next few pages is how to create a new healthy metaphorical marshmallow that you don't need to resist: so you don't use up willpower and you still achieve your dreams. This is a great motivational secret.

Before we move on...

...here's a glimpse of the marshmallow trick. Imagine that this time, before you go for your run, I ask you to note all the positive benefits you experience while running. Remember, this is entirely focused on the present moment. So forget about sensible, long-term reasons why you should run; think about the benefits you experience while moving your body.

Straight away you connect with a sense of alertness (marshmallow), you feel surprisingly more energized (marshmallow), you love chatting with your running buddy as you move (marshmallow), you feel lighter (marshmallow), you feel a sense of achievement and control over your life (marshmallow).

You've transformed the act of running as something you should do into something that's full of instant benefits – or healthy marshmallows. Rather than holding your primitive brain back from eating the I-can't-be-arsed-to-run marshmallow, you can feast on a bag of healthy marshmallows right now. No willpower required.

Hopefully you can sense the power in this switch of perspective. Because here's another secret to motivation – the motivation you need to start something is totally different from the motivation you need to keep going. Those traditional "whys" and "shoulds" will get you going, but it's the positive marshmallows that keep you showing up. And this is not fluffy positive thinking, this is how you train your primitive brain to support your goals. When you have both your primitive and human brains aligned, amazing things happen. **Change the marshmallows, change your life.**

THE MOTIVATION YOU NEED TO START SOMETHING IS TOTALLY DIFFERENT FROM THE MOTIVATION YOU NEED TO KEEP GOING

PART 2

Let's Get Ready

Chapter 5
ID Your Goal

Right now, you're going to identify one goal to focus on for the next 28 days.

From my own experience, and witnessing thousands of people transform their relationship with alcohol with a programme I'm involved with called One Year No Beer, I know that something magical can happen around the 28-day mark. There occurs the spark of a mindset shift (try saying that after a few drinks) that can transform your goal into a subconscious habit or core value – more on this in chapter 7. Basically, your goal becomes part of who you are.

By the 28th day of the motivational masterclass that I lay out in this book, your goal will either become a subconscious habit or core value, or it will be completed. Think of this whole process like a goals plunger, designed to push goals down into your subconscious (for more on this, see the goals plunger diagram on page 84). Have you ever wondered how some people find the motivation to go running every day? This is how – because **running becomes part of who they are as a person**. It has transformed into a core value so they don't have to think about running – they just find the time to do it whenever possible. Pushing a goal deep into your subconscious frees up enough mental real estate to take on your next goal until this is also part of who you are. At this point, you start on the next goal, and so on.

Maybe you've already got a specific goal in mind, and that's why you've picked up this book. Or maybe you're muddling through life feeling totally meh. You know you want to change your life, but you don't know exactly where to start.

Either way, unleashing your motivation will send that dissatisfaction packing.

SMART goals are so boring

The goal-setting process should fire you up, but it's been overtaken by the 1980s management acronym SMART. Back in 1981, when SMART goals – Specific, Measurable, Attainable, Realistic and Timed – first appeared, managers all over rejoiced. Finally, the corporate world had a way to nail their staff to specific outcomes. While SMART goals might add some value in the corporate world, in my opinion they reduce autonomy and, as we know it, motivation.

I can understand why employees are encouraged to set attainable and realistic goals to raise their chances of success. But surely the "realistic" approach to goal setting on a personal and business level is all wrong. Goal setting is about allowing yourself to dream big without reality holding you back. This does not mean you have to go large or go home. But it allows your mind to slip into the realm of what might be possible. Somewhere in the space beyond your comfort zone and before you reach the impossible zone lies the growth zone, where all the best goals reside. It is in this space that your goals can lead to deep purpose and even change the world. If everyone stuck to what they thought was realistic or achievable, we would still be in the Stone Age.

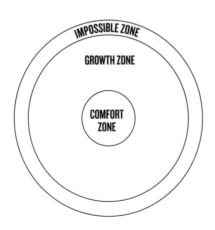

While I'm in rant mode, "attainable" and "realistic" are the same thing, all they do is help the acronym.

To be clear, I am not suggesting you have to set massive goals. The point is to give yourself the chance to mentally explore these ideas alongside your other goals. With this awareness, you can sift through your goals over the following chapters and select the one that's right for you at this moment.

So, let's get back to goal setting with a sense of freedom and fun. This is your chance to dream big without fear of being told what to do or how to act. It's an opportunity to bridge the gap between where you are and where you want to be. What could be more exhilarating than this?

You have a dream

Whether you have a clear goal in mind for the motivational masterclass or you need inspiration, the next steps will help you find that one special goal.

If you already have some resolutions or a goal you would love to conquer, now is the time to note them down. I always prefer pen and paper, as there is something powerful and visceral about physically writing out your dreams.

- I want to………..
- I want to………..
- I want to………..

Not sure? Below are some questions that might help spark a few ideas. And don't forget that goal setting is an ongoing process. At any point during the book, you might sense the tug of a new goal forming. If you do, pause and make a note of it. You can then put it in the mix when choosing your next goal.

- If money were not an issue, what would you do with your time?
- If you had a million pounds and you could only spend it on doing good in the world, what would you do with it?
- How could you use your skills to make other people's lives better?
- If you could not fail, what would you do?

Quick win

Before you go through the resolution-refiner process over the coming chapters and uncover the one golden goal you want to focus on for the next 28 days, let's score a quick win.

Quick wins appear as goals that you'd love to achieve; all they need is a little motivational boost to make them happen. Quick wins are great because they build can-do energy while saving the in-depth motivational process for your one big goal.

For example:

- To find a team sport/group class to do after work
- To go to the theatre once a month
- To organize a monthly date night

Quick wins are the sort of goals that linger at the back of your mind, but that you never find the time or energy to make happen. Well, you're different now. You can do it. To-do's don't require a full 28 days of focus – they just need a little prompting and you can tick them off nice and quickly.

Don't overthink this – just do it. Right now. Stand up, wiggle your toes, shake your legs, roll your shoulders back, lift your head. Motion is motivational emotion. Now pick up the phone, send the email and take action on at least one of your quick wins. Do this now.

I bet you feel great. Now we can move on and find that one golden goal to focus on for the next 28 days.

Why multitasking is madness

The number-one mistake you can make when setting your goals is to start them all at once. I will go further: starting any more than one goal is a mistake.

I know this is hard to grasp. There is a temptation when we set lots of goals to envisage ourselves as richer and talking fluent German while doing a handstand. We want all of this stuff now. So we jump in, start everything at once, only to see our motivation nosedive.

Let's not do that.

Running lots of goals at once can end with them all collapsing into a pile of overwhelm. Let's get this out there – we are all hopeless at multitasking. Some ingenious research from Sophie Leroy of the University of Minnesota first introduced the concept of "attention residue". When you switch tasks, your full attention doesn't follow. Part of your brain is left thinking about the previous task, which creates an attention residue. So you're not as efficient during the current task. And continually switching between tasks or multitasking builds up more and more residue, so you end up underperforming on all tasks. The antidote is found in a great book by American computer scientist Cal Newport, titled *Deep Work: Rules for Focused Success in a Distracted World*. Newport's theory is that "deep work", as he calls it – the ability to go deep on just one piece of work or goal without the distractions of the modern world – will allow you to make the breakthroughs in life and business that others can't because they are continually distracted. Newport sees "deep work" as a modern-day superpower. I agree.

We are made to mono-task. And what we already know about willpower backs this up. If you take on too many things at once your willpower reserves will quickly run dry. Result: departures from the wagon and broken dreams.

Pause. Take a deep breath. Once again, let's switch our perception of how motivation works. You are not wired to take on too many challenges at once – so don't. If you had the option either to start all your goals at once and maybe, if you were really lucky and had a fair wind behind you, achieve one goal per year; or to focus on one goal at a time for 28 days and potentially tick off your top 12 goals every year – what option would you take? It's a no-brainer, right?

So that's exactly what we will do: one goal at a time.

Chapter 6
The Six Streams of Positivity

Before you get stuck into the 28-day masterclass I want you to connect with the six streams of positivity. Sleep, movement, nutrition, connection, quiet time and clear thinking are the vital elements of wellbeing that uphold motivation. As you will discover throughout this chapter, science proves these six streams are fundamental to keeping you positive and motivated – essential when you're making a big life change.

Best of all, these streams are the elements of a life well lived. Too often we rush into those big goals and neglect life's essentials, such as hanging out with friends and getting a good night's sleep. That's why it is critical to consider the six streams before you choose the one big goal you'll focus on for the masterclass.

Before you read this chapter, I want to be clear about what's to follow. **Every time you improve one of the six streams you unleash bonus motivation.**

CASE STUDY:

SALLY DID IT!

Sally wanted to get fit, so I suggested she sleep more.

Sally's big goal was to improve her fitness and get in shape. After we reflected on her six streams of positivity, it was clear she was struggling with sleep. Poor sleep saps your mood, has a negative effect on your energy and causes the body to store fat. So the chances of getting fit while sleeping poorly are greatly reduced. Sally had never made the link between sleep, motivation and fitness.

So rather than doing what she had always done and diving into another boot-camp regime, this time we worked on improving the quality of her sleep. You can just imagine Sally thinking, "Who is this crazy ginger? I want to go to the gym and he wants me to get an early night."

Here's where the six streams flow into one another. To sleep better, Sally could reduce her alcohol intake, exercise more, eat nutritious food and create the right conditions for some quality shut-eye by having a motivational plan. It's all linked. Imagine those tributary streams flowing together and creating a river. This is the beauty of the positive streams: they all work in harmony.

So, Sally set a mini goal to improve her sleep. "Getting more sleep meant I ate a healthy breakfast instead of face-planting into a bowl of sugary cereal," she says. "And because I didn't feel so tired, I wasn't craving sweet things all afternoon." Then she turned her attention to the movement stream and guess what? "For the first time ever, I made a point of going for a big walk in my lunch hour, and I got in the habit of doing spinning and Pilates after work." She got fit fast.

Flowing with motivation, Sally then started on her next goal of saving for a new house.

Sally's story highlights why the six streams of positivity are another secret to motivation. At the end of the section about each stream, later in the chapter, you'll have the chance to give yourself a score out of ten, and on page 77 you'll find a chart to help you assess those scores. The higher your scores, the happier, more energized and more motivated you'll be to make the big changes like (in my case) switching careers, moving house or writing a book. During the 28-day masterclass you will track the individual streams and their combined motivational flow to see tangible daily progress. Bonus: being aware of your positivity stream scores might also create lots of exciting ideas about what goals you might like to achieve next.

You may be thinking that you only picked up this book because you wanted the motivation to launch a new business, and now you have to meditate, go to bed early and swap prosecco for peppermint tea. Your head may well be exploding.

Don't panic.

Breathe.

What makes my motivational masterclass different is that you will focus on one goal at a time. So, let all the wonderful ideas and goals this chapter generates float around your mind. But you don't have to action any of them just yet. I will show you how to refine your goals so you focus on just one of them for 28 days. Once this goal has been achieved, or is running as a subconscious habit, you can move on to the next goal, and so on.

Let's zoom out for a minute: you can potentially achieve your top 12 goals in one year. Imagine! You might be able to restore your marriage, transform your diet, change career, deadlift your body weight and start learning French all before midnight on 31 December, as it were.

How great would that feel?

So if your head is full of ideas, note them down. You can refine and focus on one later. Trust me: it's simple and it works. For this reason, when choosing your next motivational challenge, it is critical to reflect on your six streams of positivity, because you might want to be strategic about where you devote your attention.

By working on these positivity streams you set up the perfect foundation for lasting motivation and the most vibrant life possible.

Now let's do this.

Positivity stream #1: Sleep

We spend almost a third of our lives sleeping. And we are only just waking up to the connection between inadequate sleep and a negative impact on our mental and physical health. The real villain is that poor sleep is the enemy of motivation.

A study of New Zealand drivers suggested that five or fewer hours of sleep are comparable to mild intoxication, so if we're sleep-deprived we should not drive. There are also now tons of studies that show how poor sleep has a negative impact on mood, energy and decision-making, which are all essential ingredients for motivation.

To help my own understanding of the impact of sleep quality on motivation, I met with a man who spends a lot of time in celebrities' bedrooms. Not like that. Nick Littlehales is the author of the fantastic book *Sleep*, and has coached the Manchester United and Real Madrid soccer teams, the British Olympic team and many other uber-athletes. With his help, they have figured out that good sleep is essential to motivation and performance. And the same is true for us everyday armchair athletes, trying to be the best we can be. I see no difference between the athlete dreaming of setting a new world record and Aziza, who wants to find a new career, or Mark, who dreams of being a better role model to his kids. Winning medals is important, but being a patient father, finding that dream job and achieving your goals is just as valuable.

So here's an idea – why not approach your life the way an athlete approaches a competition? Let's start with optimizing sleep, which is the most underrated performance enhancer we have. Here, Nick shares his top three tips for quality sleep and superpower motivation:

✦ Forget the eight-hour myth. Research from Harvard Medical School demonstrates that under clinical conditions we sleep in 90-minute cycles. Each cycle consists of four to five distinct stages that we must pass through to reach deep, restorative sleep. Think of each 90-minute cycle as a flight of stairs. Over the course of 90 minutes you pass down through each stage, heading toward the bottom of the stairs where the deep-sleep phase resides, and then you walk back through the stages by climbing the stairs. You repeat this 90-minute cycle several times until you wake up. The trick is to find out roughly how many cycles you need per night. (Having allowed myself to wake up without an alarm for the period of a week, I discovered that I will naturally sleep for about 7.5 hours, which is 5 x 90-minute cycles.) Then multiply your daily number of cycles over the week to get a weekly total – in my case 5 cycles x 7 days = 35 cycles per week.

- ⫸ Nick's next tip is the big one. He suggests that sleep is not about just one night, it's about your weekly cycle total. This was really refreshing for me, because I no longer had to panic if I needed to work late, or if I got hit by one of those 2am headspins. The great irony is that by removing the pressure of getting a perfect night's sleep I actually slept better, knowing that if need be I could catch up during the week to top up my weekly total.
- ⫸ You can build up your weekly cycles by grabbing what Nick calls a Controlled Recovery Period (CRP). It's more than a nap: a CRP is a 30-minute timed rest which you can take in a quiet meeting room at the office or in the park. You don't even need to close your eyes, you just relax as if you were trying to sleep.

Ultimately, better sleep will help you achieve every single goal you have. So if you're thinking of learning a new language, running 5km (3 miles) or quitting smoking, then taking control of your sleep will support your mission. This is a major theme of this book: think tactically about your goals. Rather than jumping straight into your big burning goal, set yourself up for success by improving your positivity streams first.

UNDERSTANDING YOUR SLEEP SCORE

Score 1 if you didn't sleep at all last night
Score 2 if you barely slept – we're talking three hours or less
Score 3 if you were awake for hours in the night and now you feel like death

Score 4 if it took forever to get to sleep and you woke feeling really groggy

Score 5 if you pressed snooze twice or more this morning

Score 6 if you woke a few times in the night, but got back to sleep OK

Score 7 if...no, you can't score 7 (more about this on page 77). Think again

Score 8 if you got to bed at a decent hour and only needed one coffee today

Score 9 if you drifted off easily and slept through

Score 10 if you got to sleep within five minutes of your head hitting the pillow and woke up feeling good

Stream #2: Movement

Motion creates emotion, which fires up motivation. If you are ever struggling to find your mojo, stand up and move. It will make a difference – trust me, I know from experience. To help motivate the tough-guy City brokers I coach, I set an hourly movement alarm. When the phone chimed the whole team was encouraged (or contractually obliged) to stand up and stretch.

Over time the alarm morphed into music and I have a hysterically funny video of one of the guys, a former professional rugby player, striking poses that would make Madonna blush. Moving worked: the lads were revitalized, they made more calls and closed more deals. And it was hilarious.

Moving your body isn't a "should" or a "nice-to" – it's an unequivocal must. Whatever motivational challenge you're tackling, there is a mountain of science to show that moving your body will help.

And if exercise is just not your thing, try health by stealth. No slogging it out on the treadmill, no lifting weights. All you have to do is move your body every day in a way you enjoy, and it will make a massive difference to your fitness and your motivation. Everything counts. If you like dancing, turn up the music and start a kitchen disco. If you like walking, walk. If you enjoy gardening, get out there. When your body is moving the way it is designed to every single day, it will give you tons of extra motivation to smash your goals.

How does it work? Experts call this movement NEAT, or Non-Exercise Activity Thermogenesis. What a mouthful, so let's stick with the acronym. NEAT is essentially all the activities outside of formal exercise that burn calories, such as cleaning the house, walking to the coffee shop or running for the bus. The idea is simple – if you build more NEAT movement activities into your day, you will improve your fitness, boost your energy and build your motivation. Researcher James Levine from the Mayo Clinic in Phoenix, Arizona estimates that NEAT activities can use up a massive 350 calories per day – that's like burning off a cheeseburger. Imagine the difference that will make over time. NEAT exercise turns your world into a secret gym, one that no one knows about and where you can always get a locker!

Here are my top seven health-by-stealth movement ideas:

- **Stand at work** – if a standing desk is too big a step, take your calls standing up
- **Mix up your transport** – bike, run or walk to work. Too far? Just do the last 15 minutes of your commute
- **Get down with the kids** – you don't even have to play football. Embarrass the kids with your Ministry of Silly Walks routine, or throwing them around like kettlebells will help
- **Shop IRL, not online** – shopping in real life means moving your butt, not clicking a button
- **Kondo your cupboards** – decluttering involves heavy lifting, deep squats and hours on your feet
- **Walk and talk** – host walking meetings with teammates and take a stroll with friends instead of catching up over cake
- **Win the cleaning Olympics** – emptying the dishwasher, mopping the floor, hanging out washing: they all count

What NEAT ideas could you introduce?

UNDERSTANDING YOUR MOVEMENT SCORE

Score 1 if you haven't left the house today

Score 2 if you creak when you attempt to get up off the couch

Score 3 if you were glued to your office chair all day

Score 4 if you took the lift instead of the stairs

Score 5 if you had regular movement breaks at work and went outside at lunchtime

Score 6 if you're doing something active at the same time as reading this

Score 7 if…no, you can't score 7. Think again

Score 8 if you hit 10,000 steps

Score 9 if you inspired other people to move more too

Score 10 if you actually did more exercise today than you would have in a gym session

MOVING YOUR BODY ISN'T A "SHOULD" OR A "NICE-TO" – IT'S AN UNEQUIVOCAL MUST

Stream #3: Nutrition

Rather than pushing a meal plan on you, I will say this: the most important thing about nutrition is that you care about what you put in your mouth. Whether that's Paleo, plant-based or Mediterranean, what's important is that you're interested in the food you eat. Why? When you understand what you're eating and how that food makes you feel, you're less likely to scoff the quick and easy option.

Here's what happens when you're hungry: you're low on glucose, so the primitive brain takes control. The anxiety of blood-sugar fluctuations signals to the primitive brain that food is in short supply. It then tramples all over your sensible human goals and goes on a junk-food rampage. Result: you're distracted by the slip-up and you're not fuelling your body with real, long-lasting energy.

This is disastrous to your motivation. For example, if your goal is to sing in a band, without the right nutrition you might lose the motivation to practise. When you compound these extra nutritionally motivated practice sessions over time they can make the difference between you reaching your goal or not.

So, forget diets. Food is 100 per cent lifestyle. Eat in a way that you enjoy and that fills you with health and energy. But remember, if you have too much choice you will make poor choices. You are hard-wired by evolution to prize high-fat, high-calorie foods. You are not being weak – your primitive brain is just overpowering your rational choices and turning salads into burgers.

The best way to beat the temptations of endless choice is to align with a food tribe (I'll talk more about tribes on day 13). Knowing that you don't eat meat/processed carbs/jelly beans cuts down the options and can introduce you to a whole new healthy way of eating, while simultaneously firing up your motivation. Remember, what matters most is that you care about what you eat.

And if you want to shape up, let's not overcomplicate things: if you consume fewer calories than you burn you will drop some weight. This is where the positivity streams get interesting. If you're NEAT moving and sleeping better, you will burn extra calories. When you align with a food tribe and improve your overall nutrition, you will find your true healthy weight. Even if your goal isn't directly linked to nutrition, what you eat will help you succeed. Quality nutrition = quality motivation. Get the basics right and many of your big goals will simply fall into place.

UNDERSTANDING YOUR NUTRITION SCORE

Score 1 if you have an Everest attitude to food: "because it's there"

Score 2 if you were too busy to eat well today

Score 3 if you were at least aware that you could have picked a more nutritious option

Score 4 if you remembered to have at least one healthy snack

Score 5 if you ate at least one home-cooked meal

Score 6 if you mostly ate well, apart from that one little slip-up

Score 7 if...no, you can't score 7. Think again

Score 8 if you ate two or more meals cooked from scratch

Score 9 if you swapped an unhealthy option for fresh, nutritious food

Score 10 if you're happy with what you ate today, and you're prepped to eat well tomorrow

Stream #4: Connection

When I first ran the six positivity streams, I scored extremely low on connection. This is not a violins moment, as I feel lucky to have figured out how motivation works and my world is much brighter as a result. However, two of my best mates, Lenny and Colm, live in Ireland, which is a right hike from my home in Essex. Though I feel happily connected with my family, I miss having the lads around. Then I stumbled upon some research that was to transform my views about connection.

Social scientists have tracked the decline of our close relationships for decades by asking questions such as "How many people can you turn to in a moment of crisis or celebration?" Forty years ago, on average an American had just three close friends. The last survey, in 2014, produced by Professor Miller McPherson and his team at Duke University in North Carolina, showed that the average American now has a heart-sinking zero close friends. It can't go any lower. How sad.

I don't think it's a coincidence that, as our society cuts down on face-to-face connection, anxiety, depression and poor motivation are rising. We are social animals; we need connection to feel motivated and fulfilled. Australian author Bronnie Ware sums up the power of connection perfectly in her extraordinary memoir *The Top Five Regrets of the Dying* when she says, "There were many deep regrets about not giving friendships the time and effort that they deserved. Everyone misses their friends when they are dying."

When I run the six streams of positivity with my coaching groups, the results are the same. It's very normal for a bunch of successful, engaged, warm and friendly people to score less than five on connection. It reveals the sad truth, already discovered by social scientists, that we're becoming increasingly lonely.

Let's make this really clear: relationships are a skill we must work on. Too often we are hoodwinked into assuming our connections are what they are. That people drift apart, and that's just life. Some people are lucky to have lots of friends, while others are just solitary. I want to challenge this thinking. Everything in life can be upgraded, including your connections to the people you care about. It is up to you to leverage your motivational superpowers to make the first move. Forget the "he said, she said" or that they have not made contact with you. They are trapped by modern living, but you're breaking free. You are learning that you can control your motivational destiny. This is your time to bring meaningful connection back into your life; in so doing you will make your world brighter and your motivation will skyrocket.

Here's another secret: many of the goals you will achieve once you master motivation will improve connection. Outside your comfort zone lives all the growth, learning and increased connection to others. It's a positive motivational loop. When you think about it, connection has to form the bedrock of motivation. But it's almost entirely overlooked when setting goals. Until now.

Take the quick connection challenge

Right now, pick up the phone and call or text a special someone you have lost touch with. I guarantee you will feel better afterward, even if it takes a deep breath to be the bigger person. The bonus of this challenge is that you create the momentum that what you do matters. And that you are the guardian of your motivation.

UNDERSTANDING YOUR CONNECTION SCORE

Score 1 if you've not had face-to-face contact with anyone today

Score 2 if you cancelled plans to see friends

Score 3 if you've only had digital contact with your mates today

Score 4 if you had a quick chat with a neighbour, client or friendly face in a coffee shop

Score 5 if a colleague or acquaintance has officially moved into the friend zone

Score 6 if you've made plans to see an old friend (and you promise you won't bail)

Score 7 if…no, you can't score 7. Think again

Score 8 if you succeeded in getting friends together today

Score 9 if you caught up with a friend you hadn't seen for ages

Score 10 if you had meaningful, face-to-face chats with a few close friends today, and have more plans in your diary to look forward to

Stream #5: Quiet time

A few years ago I invited Dr Itai Ivtzan, positive psychologist and author of *Awareness is Freedom*, to teach my stressed-out City brokers mindfulness. The lads were used to my motivational techniques such as the dancing alarm, but I worried mindfulness was a step too far.

I was wrong. Dr Ivtzan's approach was perfect. He knew these guys were less about the zen and more about peak performance, and he started with a metaphor that changed the way I viewed mindfulness. "Your mind is like your smartphone," he said. "Over the course of the day you open more and more apps. The busier your world, the more apps you open, but each one reduces your phone's processing power." What happens? Your phone stops performing at its best. But, says Dr Ivtzan, "When you take a couple of minutes to clear the open apps, the phone returns to its peak. Your mind is the same.

"Over the course of the day, you build up a cognitive load that's similar to open apps on your phone, which reduces your brain capacity. You end up with a smaller percentage of mental processing power, and performance is hindered. Now imagine there is a technique that can clear your cognitive load and gift you back full processing power so you can be more productive and motivated. Well, there is and it will only take you one minute."

At this point, the lads were hooked. Dr Ivtzan showed the team a simple one-minute breathing exercise to reconnect with the present moment.

Try the one-minute zen

- Set a timer for one minute, so you're not tempted to peep at your phone until it beeps
- Breathe in through the nose for a count of four
- Breathe out through the nose to the count of four
- Stay with the counts and focus on the breath. If your mind starts to wander, gently come back to the count and the breath until your timer beeps

That's it. Simple yet super-effective.

Quiet time.

And it's not just about mindfulness. Also, simply finding a few minutes' dedicated quiet time to rest your mind will make a massive difference to your motivation. You might pray, close your eyes or just sit in a quiet space. The resulting peace is the same. When you allow your mind to rest, it can bounce back stronger.

UNDERSTANDING YOUR QUIET TIME SCORE

Score 1 if you haven't stopped all day and your head is absolutely spinning

Score 2 if you checked social media or email the minute you woke up

Score 3 if you did try to pause and breathe, but got distracted

Score 4 if you managed to concentrate on a problem and unravel it in your head

Score 5 if you paused for a full minute today without jumping on your phone

Score 6 if you read a book or looked out the window on your commute instead of checking your email

Score 7 if...no, you can't score 7. Think again

Score 8 if you paused in a busy place and sat in stillness as chaos whirled around you

Score 9 if you took a walk or practised yoga and resisted the urge to grab your phone

Score 10 if you took several different pauses today – walking, reading, mindfulness – and feel peaceful now

Stream #6: Clear thinking

From my own experience and being lucky enough to have seen thousands of others do the same, I know the difference that taking a break from drinking can make to clear thinking and, with it, motivation.

And I know what you're thinking: Sergeant Bore-Off of the fun police has arrived to steal your fun. But the opposite is true. My mission is to help you achieve your dreams – what could be more fun and exciting than that?

I am not talking about giving up booze forever. I'm talking about reducing the volume or using tactical breaks to test how you feel. And if you feel energized and motivated, then why not keep going?

So please walk with me on this one, because it is vital we have this conversation. No one else wants to say it. Almost all coaches, trainers, influencers and motivational individuals wax lyrical about many of the other positivity streams, but ignore the pint-shaped elephant in the room – alcohol. Why? Because they drink themselves. But I want to focus on those clear-thinking heroes who are crushing it because they have made the connection between alcohol and motivation. Beyonce, Ollie Ollerton (former Special Forces soldier and star of the TV show *SAS: Who Dares Wins*) and Bradley Cooper are a few examples of those who are living the alcohol-free dream.

In my opinion, the two streams that produce the quickest and most influential effect on your motivation are alcohol and sleep. If you deal with these two things, your motivation will skyrocket. The beauty is, like all the motivational streams, sleep and alcohol are connected. Research shows that alcohol destroys the deep, restorative phase of sleep, so, if you think back to Nick Littlehales' metaphor, you never reach the bottom of the stairs. Even a few glasses will interrupt your natural sleep patterns, which reduces daytime alertness, saps productivity and therefore erodes your motivation.

Clear thinking is a superpower motivational stream because it will unlock your consistency in everything from moving your body to eating better.

I cannot overstate the importance of consistency. If you can show up enough times and perform your daily goal task, whether that's to write 500 words, run 5km (3 miles) or make ten client calls, you will achieve your dreams. It's that simple. And alcohol muddies that clarity of thought with a great big cloud of can't-be-arsed. Suddenly you miss the run, skip the 500 words, put off making the calls and your goal momentum is lost. But when you remove alcohol you think clearly and get consistent: you find the motivation to keep turning up day after day. And it is the small daily wins that make magic things happen.

One last thing on the alcohol subject: there's nothing to "give up" and tons of motivation to gain, and it's yours for the taking.

UNDERSTANDING YOUR CLEAR THINKING SCORE

Score 1 if all you think about is when you can have your next drink

Score 2 if you were hungover today, and you're back on the beers tonight

Score 3 if you're still recovering from a big night out two days later

Score 4 if you were doing OK until a friend lured you into the pub

Score 5 if you stayed under the official approved limit for drinking (14 units a week: that's seven glasses of wine or six pints of beer)

Score 6 if you've only had one or two drinks this week

Score 7 if…no, you can't score 7. Think again

Score 8 if you honestly feel "take it or leave it" about booze

Score 9 if you resist a drink-pusher and have fun without a glass in your hand

Score 10 if you've been alcohol-free for 28 days or more, and you're happy to be free

ALCOHOL MUDDIES THAT CLARITY
OF THOUGHT WITH A GREAT BIG
CLOUD OF CAN'T-BE-ARSED

Your Six Streams Scores

Imagine that each of the six columns below represents a stream that supports your motivational flow; more importantly they combine into a torrent that takes you toward a life well lived. Not only do these streams keep your primitive brain happy, they also combine to gift you extra motivation. How do you score?

SCORE YOUR SIX POSITIVITY STREAMS:

#1 Sleep	#2 Movement	#3 Nutrition	#4 Connection	#5 Quiet time	#6 Clear thinking
1	1	1	1	1	1
2	2	2	2	2	2
3	3	3	3	3	3
4	4	4	4	4	4
5	5	5	5	5	5
6	6	6	6	6	6
7	7	7	7	7	7
8	8	8	8	8	8
9	9	9	9	9	9
10	10	10	10	10	10

From now on I want you to think about the six streams of positivity on a daily basis, as these are the basics of motivation. The results will help you track your progress and reveal any areas that need work.

What do you do? For each stream, simply score how you feel today. Ten means you're flying and one suggests this area requires serious attention.

One caveat: you can't score a seven. Lucky number seven is an easy option. Picking six or eight forces you to think more deeply about your choices. What we're trying to achieve is a very visual representation of where you're at with these foundational motivational elements.

Everything is connected

Hopefully, the message is shining through that the six positivity streams are not only the foundation of your motivation, but also the gateway to fulfilment and happiness.

For too many years I was guilty of chasing goals that looked great on paper, while totally neglecting the most vital goal streams of all: sleep, movement, nutrition, connection, quiet time and clear thinking.

So before you dash into the 28-day challenge, think like a motivational pro and get tactical with your goals.

Stack the goals in your favour

Now you know about the six streams of positivity, use your scores as a guide to deciding which big goal you want to tackle first. Be tactical. You might want to start with a goal that will improve one of your six streams. Because, as you now know, the higher these scores, the higher your chances of finding the motivation you need to achieve your other goals.

Here is a great example from one of my masterclass members. Jimmy's goals looked like this:

- Save for a house
- Learn Spanish
- Get fit
- Eat better

When Jimmy ran the six streams of positivity, he produced the following scores: *3/1/20*

Sleep	6	8
Movement	2	5
Nutrition	5	8
Connection	8	4
Quiet time	6	9
Clear thinking	8	5

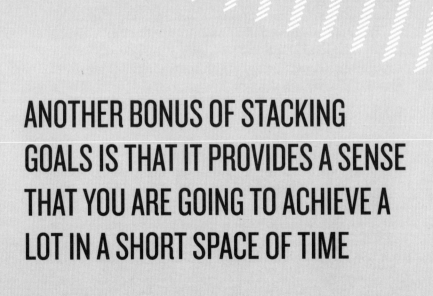

ANOTHER BONUS OF STACKING
GOALS IS THAT IT PROVIDES A SENSE
THAT YOU ARE GOING TO ACHIEVE A
LOT IN A SHORT SPACE OF TIME

It was now obvious to Jimmy that his lack of movement was potentially holding him back, and was perhaps a contributing factor to his lack of motivation to save for a house. He adjusted his list to include new movement goals to maximize momentum. He then stacked the rest of his goals to increase his six stream scores, before taking on his more traditional goals.

Jimmy's revised goals looked like this:

- Daily movement – cycle to work, use the stairs in the office, weekly yoga
- Quality sleep – be in bed by 11pm every night
- Eat better – quit processed food and cook from scratch
- Save for a house – put aside 20 per cent of my income
- Learn Spanish – I want to speak it before I fly to Mexico

Being tactical and stacking his goals provided Jimmy with motivational momentum that made each subsequent goal easier to achieve. He figured that once his body was moving every day, he would sleep better and find it easier to get fit. Sleep and movement would provide extra motivation to stick with his new healthy-eating regime. Feeling fitter, slimmer and more energized, Jimmy knew the chances of him taking on his big goal to save for a house were increased exponentially.

Another bonus of stacking goals is that it provides a sense that you are going to achieve a lot in a short space of time. As we've already discovered, starting all your goals at once doesn't work. So stacking them creates a sense of doing lots while allowing you to focus on just one goal at a time.

If you get stuck, these filter questions can reveal your top goal to focus on for the rest of the book:

- Is this a goal you would love to start today?
- Would this goal be better served by achieving other goals first?
- Does this goal improve any of your positivity streams? If so, which ones?
- What will the improvements to your positive streams do for you?
- Will working toward this goal make it easier to achieve more goals?

• Can this goal benefit others?

Before we move on, just imagine that within a few months everything in your life will improve. You might find that perfect job and see your stress levels plummet as your diet changes and you move your body on a daily basis. Perhaps you'll drop a dress size and see your health blossom and your skin glow. With stress reduced you might work on your sleep, which fuels a healthier mindset so you're more energized and confident to join the running club. Maybe you'll find a deep connection with your running tribe, which leads to meaning and purpose as you uncover a love for the outdoors. Now you're thriving again. And most importantly, you're feeling happy.

Does this mean that all of life's ups and downs level out? No. But you are now living a life that is full of vibrancy and meaning, so when the tough times come you will be more resilient and bounce back quicker. This is the power of the six streams and owning your motivational plan.

Chapter 7
The Goals Plunger

Over the next 28 days, you will complete a motivational masterclass. The idea is that after that time you will either reach your goal or create a habitual process that will continue to run until you achieve your dream.

So, to be very clear, this does not mean your goal has to be complete within 28 days. What it does mean is that after these four weeks you will have formed a plan that will allow your goal to run as a subconscious habit or core value. Once you're performing your daily goal task on autopilot because it's embedded in your subconscious, you will free up the mental real estate to move on to your next goal until this is also running as a habit or core value.

For example, if your goal is to run a marathon that's six months away, you would use the masterclass to build the daily plan and habits necessary to hit your running quota. The idea is that, after you've reached the 28-day mark, your marathon goal will take care of itself. You will have formed a daily running motivation plan that you can just execute without thinking. At this point, you can turn your major focus to your next goal for 28 days until this also runs on autopilot.

Another example for you: my friend Colm's goal was to be able to play his favourite song on the guitar. After 28 days he hadn't reached his goal, but he had created a powerful daily habit of practising. His goal task to practise was now running on autopilot as part of his motivational morning routine. So he was ready to move on to his next goal of starting a diploma in coaching. For the following 28 days, his main focus was on creating a motivational plan for his studying. At the end of that time, he was running both his guitar practice and his studying as habitual routines. These habits were chugging away in the background, moving ever closer to his dream of strumming "Stairway to Heaven" and becoming a coach. Meanwhile, Colm could focus on any other goals he wished to achieve.

The 28-day motivational masterclass outlined in this book is designed to push one goal at a time down through your willpower layers into your subconscious, where it is embedded into the very core of your identity.

You can imagine motivational layers like this:

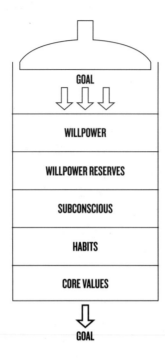

Willpower sits on the top layer with its nemesis, ambivalence. You know ambivalence – it's when you have mixed feelings about your actions. On the one hand, you really want to go to the gym, but on the other, you would love to stay on the couch. A large part of the motivational masterclass is designed to eliminate ambivalence.

Willpower is not found in the subconscious layers because there is no longer ambivalence. At these depths, your motivational challenges become subconscious habits or core values. The aim of the masterclass is to push your goal deep into the core of your identity, so it becomes part of who you are. When your goal exists in there, ambivalence can't mess with it.

Habits are great, but values are ten times better

Don't get me wrong, I love a good habit, but healthy routines are always in danger of getting bulldozed by unhealthy ones. Therefore, wherever possible, we want to make our goals into core values. But before that can happen, we need to make each goal a habit. The motivational dream is that, over time, this habit becomes part of who we are and moves deeper into a core value. At this point, motivation is no longer required. We just perform the daily goal tasks because they are part of our very soul.

Let's first learn how to create a habit. In his book *The Power of Habit*, Charles Duhigg explains, "To change a habit, you must keep the old cue, and deliver the old reward, but insert a new routine."

For example, a smoker might have an 11am break, which is their trigger. The reward might be chatting to their friends and catching up on some juicy office gossip. The old routine was to achieve this reward by smoking.

So, to change the habit, the plan would be to keep the 11am trigger and the reward of a chat, but swap the smoking routine for a healthier one. In this example, a cup of coffee. This gives the hands something to do and creates a little buzz, while the former smoker can still find out who is making out with whom.

Swapping habit routines really works. If you play the new healthy routine enough times, the unhealthy habit of smoking is pushed out. But at the habit level, the smoking routine sits in the background, ready to fire given half a chance. It's like never forgetting how to ride a bike. For this reason we are vulnerable to a bad habit hijacking.

We have all unwound a good habit when ambushed by circumstances that we were not prepared for. Imagine the former smoker arriving for the 11am break and finding the coffee machine broken. Without them thinking, the old routine rears up, and a restless hand reaches for a cigarette. They are a smoker again.

Compare this to another smoker who replaced the smoking habit routine with a healthy one, but took it further. Over time the new habit of not smoking became a core value. Smoking was no longer part of who they were. Lighting up would be a violation of their deepest held beliefs about health. They don't see themselves as a former smoker – they just don't smoke. Why would they? If the coffee machine is broken, it's irrelevant. They go without coffee.

You can see the power that a core value offers. It takes a habit and moves it into a place that's protected by both your human and your primitive brain, so it can't be hijacked by the old unhelpful habits.

The masterclass you are about to undertake is designed to push your goals as far into your subconscious as possible. We want your primitive brain to fully accept and embrace your dreams. This is not just about replacing habits, it's also about creating new ones and pushing these into the core value layer too.

You could argue that some goals might only ever become a habit – for example, learning to play the guitar. But why stop there? Why not make music a fundamental part of who you are? If playing the guitar becomes an expression of your identity, you are much more likely to practise every day. To the point that you won't feel like yourself without your guitar.

Let's take physical movement. You can quickly build a daily movement habit. But how many times have you started exercise, getting on a great streak for a few weeks or months, before life becomes too busy, you miss a few sessions and the habit is broken?

Compare this to someone who has followed the masterclass to such an extent that movement is as fundamental to their lives as breathing. If this person misses a few days, they pick it up at the next opportunity. Or they adapt their new routine around their life. Instead of going to the usual 60-minute class, they might choose to walk to a meeting or bust out a HIIT session in the garage. Whatever happens, moving their body is something they deeply value, so it will always be a part of their life. This habit will not be broken because it is established at the core of their being.

If you can leverage this masterclass to turn all your big goals into core values, perhaps you will become someone who is effortlessly fit, eats healthily, has great connections and sleeps well. Not because you should, but because it's part of who you are. This is where you will find endless motivation.

Own your goal

What can sport teach us about motivation? At Euro 96 – the European soccer championship – England player Gareth Southgate missed a semi-final penalty that sent his team home. Imagine the pain. Southgate discovered the hard way that, when you don't take control of the plan, you're too easily influenced by things outside your control – the crowd, the opposition, worrying what people will say. These outside forces can penetrate your mind and destroy performance. Nerves take hold and a shot is missed.

Fast-forward to the 2018 World Cup quarter-final and Gareth was back in a penalty shootout, this time as the England manager.

To prepare for the World Cup he had hired one of the world's leading sports psychologists, Dr Pippa Grange. Her mission was to help each player form a plan to handle any high-pressure moments. Players rehearsed and visualized taking control of the penalty to build their mental resilience for the big moment. They owned every stage, from the pace they walked toward the penalty spot to where they placed the ball, how they managed their breathing and the direction of their shot. Rather than the moment owning them, they were prepared to own the moment.

When England drew with Colombia there was only one way to settle the match: penalties. The whole country was poised for England to lose. At 3-3 the Colombians missed their chance to take the lead. Eric Dier stepped up, followed the plan – and scored, launching England into the quarter-finals. Just minutes after England's first ever penalty victory, Gareth Southgate summed it up: "We had talked long and hard about owning the process of a shootout." By owning the motivational process, the England team had taken control, without having to think. They just pressed "play" and executed the plan.

Your motivational challenge might not involve a ball and thousands of cheering fans, but the principles remain the same. By taking full ownership of your challenge, you can metaphorically score your goal.

Monkeying around

Inspired by Gareth Southgate and Pippa Grange, I once again dived into the research, found another scientist who filled the blanks in my knowledge, and unlocked a motivational plan that would *actually* change my life.

Let me introduce Harry Harlow. Back in 1949 Harlow, a pioneering psychologist, created the world's first laboratory to study primate behaviour. During one of these monkey tests, in 1950, motivation took an unexpected turn.

Harlow and his colleagues devised a series of mechanical puzzles to test primate learning. To prepare the monkeys for the tests, the researchers thought it wise to leave one of the puzzles in each cage for a couple of weeks. They weren't expecting the monkeys to care about the puzzles, as there were no rewards or punishment attached. They just wanted them to feel comfortable having the puzzles in the cages. What happened next left the scientists baffled.

Rather than ignore the puzzles, the monkeys began playing with them. To solve each puzzle they had to remove a vertical pin, unlock a latch and release a mechanical hinge. With focus, determination and almost a smile on their faces, the monkeys figured out how to do all these things. This made no sense. Why were they appearing to enjoy completing the puzzles when there was no associated reward?

This behaviour did not fit the scientific model at the time. Up until this point it was widely believed that monkeys and other ape-like creatures (including humans) were only motivated to satisfy their biological drive for water, food, sex and sleep. So this peculiar monkey behaviour was totally unexpected.

It was clear that, without any external motivators, the monkeys had gained significant learning and had reached a high level of performance. They were solving puzzles because they enjoyed it. They were choosing to do the work because it was fun. The pleasure of working out the problem was fuelling their motivation. Harlow speculated that this intrinsic or internal motivation could be a missing drive. To test his emerging theory, he decided to put intrinsic motivation head to head with biological and evolutionary motivation, the assumption being that the two known motivational drives of biology and evolution would supersede the potentially new intrinsic one.

To Harlow's astonishment, the monkeys performed worse when motivated with the reward of raisins. They made more mistakes and were slower to complete the mechanical puzzle. Like Newton's apple, this was a reality-shifting discovery, as author and political speechwriter Dan Pink explains in his genius book *Drive*: "It was akin to rolling a steel ball down an inclined plane to measure its velocity – only to watch the ball float into the air instead."

Harlow and his team had stumbled upon a new intrinsic motivational drive that worked just as well for humans as it did for monkeys. What's more, Harlow reported that this internal motivation might "represent a form of motivation which may be as primary and as important as the homeostatic drives". The motivational game was afoot.

Self-determination

Building on what Harlow discovered back in 1950, two more researchers, Richard Ryan and Edward Deci, both professors at the University of Rochester, New York, picked up the intrinsic baton and created a new theory – in my opinion the greatest theory of motivation: self-determination theory (SDT).

Ever since the cognitive revolution about 70,000 years ago, when we grew our new human brain, the system of reward and punishment had worked perfectly. The idea was simple: to motivate someone, you dangled a carrot or hit them with a stick. If motivation faded, you produced a bigger prize or harsher punishment. But in the 20th century the carrot and stick appeared to stop working.

OK, I'm exaggerating slightly, so let me put it another way. Reward and punishment still work for certain tasks, but motivation has evolved to include another level that even the biggest carrots and heaviest sticks won't influence. We have started to crave something more.

Ryan and Deci's research confirmed what Harlow and his monkeys already knew: pursuing goals because you enjoy them is a powerful motivator. We have an inbuilt yearning for ownership over our actions. In SDT it's called autonomy. "To be autonomous means to behave with a sense of volition, willingness, and congruence; it means to fully endorse and concur with the behavior one is engaged in," write Ryan and Deci.

In other words, you feel autonomous (able to determine your own actions based on your values and beliefs) when you pursue goals that you *want* to achieve.

When you think about it, we're all inquisitive creatures who love to explore and absorb information without need for punishment or reward. Growing up I loved to play football, knit scarves with my nan and go birdwatching – though I admit that the last two were done in secret. As an adult I adore writing and (don't tell the publisher) money didn't motivate me to write this book. I am doing it because I love trying to distil complex ideas into easy-to-understand language. I love working my own hours, doing my own research and typing away in a coffee shop looking a little bit mysterious.

Obvious as autonomous behaviour seems, it had been totally overlooked by the scientific community. Prior to Ryan and Deci, existing research focused solely on how much motivation someone did or didn't have. As the new kids on the block, Ryan and Deci discovered that knowing whether motivation felt autonomous or controlled was a much better predictor of engagement, performance and wellbeing. Essentially they were the first to show two types of motivation – extrinsic (controlled), as in the carrot and stick, and the upgraded intrinsic (autonomous), where you choose to do something because you want to.

What doubles the importance of this research is that not only is autonomy a major motivator, it supersedes the more simplistic concept of punishment and reward. The motivational game has officially changed. The carrot and stick are no longer enough. It's time for a new approach to motivation. One that will give you total ownership over your goals, because **you will do the work that's required because you want to, not because you feel as if you should**.

Chapter 8

I Love It When a Plan Comes Together

A common motivational mistake is to focus all attention on the end result of achieving a goal, which is like looking up at Everest and wondering how the hell you are going to climb that. When you feel dwarfed by the size of your challenge, it can be overwhelming. Result: motivation trickles away.

It is critical to remember that setting goals is totally separate from the motivational plan required to achieve them. Often, finding a goal is the easy part. Turning up every day in an effort to attain it is where it gets tricky.

Our joint mission for the rest of this book is to create a plan that you own and that you can follow to ensure that you do what you have to do. No one sprints up Everest in one day. To reach the summit of the mountain, you must know where you're heading and then add up lots of little climbs to reach the top. The motivational plan you create is like a personal accountability centre that will keep you showing up and making each little climb. When you master the plan you will achieve your goals.

If you don't have a plan...

...someone, something or evolution will have a plan for you. Evolution's plan is simple: survive long enough to reproduce. That's it. Sharks, zebras, rabbits, ladybirds and humans are all motivated by the same evolutionary force. As psychologist Douglas Lisle explains in his book *The Pleasure Trap*, "For more than three thousand million years, creatures have battled, bitten, strutted, and stalked in a timeless and mysterious competitive dance." We are here because our ancestors kept fighting the good fight to stay alive long enough to get their genes into the next generation.

Most of this evolutionary excitement happens below the radar. Every single organism on this planet, including you, is doing the same survival dance. But this evolutionary magic show is hidden within the primitive part of our brains. Yes, we know all about those sexual urges, and the need for food and warmth. But in general these inner evolutionary workings are guiding our choices without us really knowing.

The emotional goalposts

Evolution executes its cunning plan through a system of what Lisle calls "emotional goalposts", also known as pleasure, pain and energy maintenance. Eating, sleeping and having sex feel good. Whereas breaking a leg, being hungry, not having a mate, missing an episode of your favourite show or being thrown out of the tribe feels bad.

For millennia, humans, like the rest of the animal kingdom, had their true north perfectly illuminated by these emotional lights. The rabbit requires energy to flee from the fox to avoid the pain of being attacked or eaten. If the rabbit is quick enough, it might experience the pleasure of eating the farmer's carrots and breeding like a rabbit. By following the motivational goalposts, every living breathing thing has the same plan: to reproduce its genes by moving away from pain toward pleasure.

Here's the thing, and it's important to connect with this: our current evolutionary kit is no different from the rabbits' and sharks'. Evolution did not catch a peep of the specimen before her in the mirror this morning, drop the mic and stroll off the stage of life with the words, "My work here is done."

No, your evolutionary hardware is running right now, motivating you to do things at a subconscious level that always serve the same purpose – survive long enough to get your genes into the next generation.

Who moved the emotional goalposts?

When we stopped hunting and gathering, around 30,000 years ago, and started to domesticate animals and plants, our evolutionary hardware was hopelessly out of date. The self-serving tweaks to our genetic code started to misfire. We could no longer rely on the emotional goalposts of pleasure, pain and energy conservation to guide us. It was like relying on Google maps to get to a meeting, using a map of the wrong city.

Back in the good old hunter-gatherer days, a doughnut would have shone like evolutionary gold, so we would have wanted it

– badly. Even today, to our primitive brain, the sweet halo is filled with high-sugar, energy-producing, life-saving pleasure. So begins the eternal ambivalence battle with the subconscious saboteur whom you will meet on day 9 of the masterclass. Your primitive brain wants a doughnut. Your human brain wants to avoid it. A tug-of-war ensues that too often ends up with a victory to the primitive brain. You're left dazed and perplexed: how did you end up eating the doughnut when you're supposed to be on a diet? And food is just the start.

Most things in life that are holding you back are linked to a misfiring motivational system. Remember, if you don't have a plan, evolution has one for you – and so does everyone else.

Let me expand on this. How many times have you woken up to the email, text, last-minute panic, missing lunchbox, work deadline or problem that someone "needs" you to solve? These people aren't trying to be mean: this is life. "Can you please do this for me, or would you mind doing that…?" It happens almost every single day. And the result: we dive head first into survival mode. Suddenly we are doing our best to get through the day. Trying to juggle work, family, stress and the ever-growing demands of other people. And as you will find out on day 23, microbes that live in your gut also have a plan for you.

Too often our motivational challenges are pushed out and forgotten, only to resurface at the stroke of midnight on 31 December. At which point we promise that next year will be different.

Paradoxically, the only way to live a spontaneous life is to plan it. As you are about to discover, there is freedom in the plan.

So, what's the plan?

- Set up the daily rituals so you do not have to think, you just *do*
- Create your own personal accountability centre that will keep you showing up every day

THE ONLY WAY TO LIVE A SPONTANEOUS LIFE IS TO PLAN IT

Three steps to create your daily rituals

As soon as you wake, the motivational plan begins with a morning ritual. Where possible avoid any tech and find five minutes' space to work with your journal. (In case journaling is new to you, I'll explain what this involves in this section.) You might like a cup of tea or a shower before you begin. The key, as always, is that you use this masterclass as your guide, but ultimately you take total ownership of your morning ritual.

The morning ritual is followed by the second step, which is to take action to execute your specific daily goal task. Finally you perform the evening ritual, which closes the accountability loop by having you answer a simple question before bed.

But journaling doesn't work for me

If you have tried journaling before and it didn't work for you, please try this format. It is deliberately super-focused, quick and powerful.

The critical point is that every morning you connect with who you are, the goal you're aiming for and the steps you'll take to get there. I will show you how to do this via the rituals I have tried and tested, both myself and with thousands of my masterclass coaching members. The journal is a vehicle to make these rituals more powerful by physically writing them out.

But if journaling is really not for you, try following the rituals in your head by mentally performing the journaling process, perhaps in front of the mirror after you brush your teeth, or by typing it out on your phone. I cannot say this too often: you need a daily plan. Winging it doesn't work. It is fundamental that you take ownership of and follow the morning and evening rituals to hold *you* accountable to your dreams. Here's what to do:

This is not "dear diary" journaling

What I've discovered about journaling is that if it's not super-simple and quick, people don't do it. So I have cut away all the fluff. Your aim is simple: reconnect on a daily basis with who you are, what goal you're heading for and how you're going to get there. It only takes two minutes so, yes, you do have time.

Take a fresh page and draw a stepped line like the one below. Imagine these are the "moon steps" you're taking toward your goal.

At the top of the stairs, draw a circle to represent the 28-day goal you've set. That's your "moonshot". Write your goal above the circle.

At the bottom, put the date by which you wish to complete your goal. Don't worry if it's longer than 28 days. As you discovered with the goals plunger (see page 82), the aim is to create a plan that will push the moon steps you require to reach your goal into a habit or subconscious value. At this point you will be performing the goal steps habitually, so you can then move on to your next goal and so on.

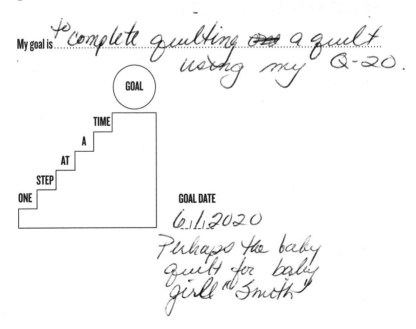

My goal is *Complete quilting on a quilt using my Q-20.*

GOAL

TIME
A
AT
STEP
ONE

GOAL DATE
6.1.2020
Perhaps the baby quilt for baby girl "Smith"

By physically writing your goal down every day, you reconnect with it both consciously and subconsciously. The act of writing proves this goal is of value. The subconscious mind uses the goals you set to filter information. This is why you will start to see the people, resources and things you need to achieve your goals. The law of attraction is based on these principles.

However (I will soon need a caveat for my caveats) this is not an exact science, so some goals may require longer to move into your core. For example, stopping drinking, in my experience, takes between 28 and 90 days to move into a core value. Equally, some goals will take less than 28 days. So let's just say on average over the year your goals will take 28 days to become a subconscious habit or value. You can adapt as you see fit for each goal.

Ask the morning power question

Below the goal step triangle you've drawn in your journal write the question, "What can I do today to improve my motivational process?"

Now, answer the question.

If your goal is to save £100 per month, your step today might be to stay within a certain spend limit. If your goal is to write a novel, today's mission might be to bash out 500 words.

By answering the daily morning power question you take charge of the process. The question makes you think about how *you* can ensure that *you* perform the routine required to reach your goal. This is so simple but unbelievably powerful because you are always taking ownership of your motivation.

Ask the evening question

At the end of the day, look back over what you've achieved and close your daily rituals with a question: *Did I do my best to [insert goal step] today?*

The key to an evening check-in ritual is that it's even shorter than your morning one. The simpler the better. At the end of each day, all you have to do is ask the evening question and give yourself a mark out of ten, with ten being a perfect score and zero being a total flop. Oh, and once again, you can't score a seven.

You will find this process tough and motivating at the same time. Scoring yourself out of ten makes you think about whether or not *you* made the effort to follow your motivational plan. Based on this score you can tweak your process the following day when you ask the morning power question – what can I do today to improve my plan? And the evening ritual will take about 60 seconds. Easy.

You're also going to score your six streams of positivity daily, so you can see tangible improvements in your motivation foundation. When I was working on writing this book, my journal entries looked like this:

My goal is .... **Write book** ....

GOAL

Marshmallows
I get into flow
Love creating new ideas

STEP ONE • AT • A • TIME

GOAL DATE
31/6/19

Give yourself a kick-start

Think of your daily rituals as being like your personal motivational coach. They hold you accountable. It's like having me banging on your door every morning to fire you up, and checking in on you before bed.

I want you to imagine that every morning when you open your journal you're powering up a motivational force field. Feel free to go all science fiction and make your force field bright colours or a translucent liquid. Now imagine that anything that tries to steal your motivation will be deflected. Those annoying emails will bounce away; your primitive brain's demand to stay in your comfort zone won't get through.

Inside your motivational bubble, it's powerful yet peaceful. You're in control. Breathe deeply. You feel relaxed, alert. You know exactly who you are, where you're going and how you're going to get there. You have the skills to deal with all life has to throw at you. You are laser-focused on the steps required to achieve your goals.

If you take just one thing from this book, creating a motivational force field via a morning and evening ritual that brackets your day with intention will change your world.

Remember, if you don't have a plan, someone or something else has one for you.

The morning and evening questions create a virtuous cycle of accountability, action and motivation. Plus you cannot turn up every day and go through this process without taking any action toward your goal. Very quickly you will have to rethink and select a new goal or, in the most positive way, get off your butt and take action. Genius.

From now onward, you're going to follow these rituals every day. Let's do this.

Sometimes real progress is scary

If there is a part of you that wants to run from the whole process – pause, and know it's because you're scared. This is how I felt when I first experimented with these ideas. Because for the first time in a long time I knew I might actually achieve my goals, but I also realized that it was going to take a lot of daily effort to get there. Please don't use the excuse that you can't do it, because you can. If you really want this goal, come back to the plan and keep showing up for 28 days until it's done. The choice is yours.

Let that last sentence sink in.

The choice is yours to reach your goal or not. It has nothing to do with time, ability, luck, work, other people, the government or money. The choice is yours to show up every day and do the work that's required. If this goal is what you really want, the daily plan will help you make it happen.

What if I miss a ritual?

There will be days when rituals get missed and stumbles happen. But trips, blips and missed days are all part of your motivational learning process. Don't run from them. Embrace missed days as a chance to be better the following day.

Developing rituals is like building any habit. It will stick through repetition. Show up enough times and it will become part of who you are. You will become someone who starts and ends their day with intention and who consistently makes progress toward their goals.

On day 2 of the masterclass, I will show you a neat trick to piggyback existing triggers to set up your goals routine. This same technique will work perfectly for triggering your morning and evening routines. Having the courage to stick with the rituals and tweak the plan until it's right will help you to successfully achieve your goal. And the next one. And the one after that.

But I don't have time for the plan

You do. Everyone has two minutes. If your goal is important, make time. Let's not hide behind the "time" excuse. On day 3, we will jump into a time machine and I will show you that you have a lot more time than you think.

THE DAILY MOTIVATIONAL PLAN IN A NUTSHELL

MORNING RITUAL

- WAKE UP
- BEFORE ANY TECH, WRITE YOUR MOON SHOT IN YOUR JOURNAL
- ANSWER THE POWER QUESTION, "WHAT CAN I DO TODAY TO IMPROVE MY MOTIVATIONAL PROCESS?"

EVENING RITUAL

- ASK THE EVENING QUESTION, "DID I DO MY BEST TO [INSERT GOAL] TODAY?" SCORE YOURSELF OUT OF TEN

Why your goals will never be the same again

Unlike conventional goal setting, which requires you to start with a blank page each time you set a new goal, you will soon own a motivational plan that works for *every* goal. To achieve your next goal, all you do is execute a different daily goal step; the plan of journaling combined with the morning and evening rituals stays the same.

Once the rituals become habit, it gets easier and easier to find the motivation to crush your goals. After 28 days you can select your next goal and simply drop it into your existing motivational plan and follow the rituals.

SIX STREAMS OF POSITIVITY

RATE THESE OUT OF TEN FOR THE DAY (REMEMBER, NO SEVENS)

THE ACCOUNTABILITY LOOP

BASED ON YOUR ANSWER TO THE EVENING QUESTION AND YOUR SIX STREAMS OF POSITIVITY, TWEAK THE PLAN TO CONSISTENTLY PERFORM YOUR DAILY GOAL STEP... AND SO ON, UNTIL YOU REACH YOUR MOONSHOT.

#1. Sleep   4. Connection
2. Movement   5. Quiet Time
3. Nutrition   6. Clear Thinking

IF THE TRAINER DID NOT SHOW UP, YOU COULD PERFORM THE WHOLE SESSION WITHOUT THEM

Now it's time for you to own it

The mistake that 99.9 per cent of all fitness coaches make is that they want *you* to follow *their* plan. To an extent, this can work. But what happens when the sessions stop? Too often all momentum is lost because you did not own the plan yourself. So when you have to go it alone, you're lost. Remember, motivation is a skill that you can learn. It is not something that other people give you. It is yours to master.

Now imagine the coach did what I am about to do, and encouraged you to create and tweak the plan so you build it together. You would understand how the machines worked, why you were performing a certain number of reps, what weight you were lifting and the types of exercise you enjoyed. If the trainer did not show up, you could perform the whole session without them. This is what I mean by owning your motivational plan. And, as we know, autonomy is the secret sauce to long-term motivation.

Try to imagine the next 28 days as our one-to-one time, where we create the plan that you own, based on a framework I'll show you. It is then up to you to own it and turn up enough times to reach your goal. Let's do this.

PART 3

Let's Do This – the 28-Day Masterclass

The 28-day masterclass you're about to experience will show you exactly how to master your motivation by helping you to create a unique plan that you take full ownership of. Every day is designed to build on the next, creating the momentum you will need to transform your goal steps into subconscious habits or values that will run on autopilot. At the end of the 28 days, you will have mastered the motivation required to achieve your goal and be ready to take on your next goal.

My goal is: *learn How to use Q-20.*

And 28 days from now, I will have mastered my motivation.

to quilt.

Week 1 – Ignite the Spark of Motivation

You know your goal. So you need a plan that motivates you to perform the daily steps required to achieve this goal. If your goal is to shape up, the daily step is to move your body; when you climb enough steps you'll be fit. If your aim is to learn Spanish, your daily step is to practise vocabulary; when you climb enough steps you'll be fluent.

Week 1 is designed to ignite the spark of motivation. You'll set up your motivational plan, so you don't have to think – you just do. By the end of week 1 you will be motivated to show up and climb your daily step.

Let's do this.

DAY 1: STREAK WITH A TWIST

Success doesn't just magically happen. Look at Jerry Seinfeld, star and co-writer of the phenomenal sitcom *Seinfeld*. Behind the comedy genius is a motivational plan that has kept Jerry at the top of his game.

How? Seinfeld realized early on that the secret to comedy was to write better jokes, and the way to get better jokes was to turn up every day and write them. So he wrote a new joke every day, and to fire up motivation he put a big red "X" on his wall calendar each time he stuck to the plan. After a few days he built up some momentum and then his mission was simple: don't break the chain or, in other words, keep the winning streak going. The longer the streak of successive days, the more motivated Jerry was to not lose his winning streak or break the chain.

The daily dedicated practice of keeping the streak going helped him consistently stay at the top of his game and earn billions of dollars.

Seinfeld instinctively knew what research from the Universities of Sheffield, Leeds and North Carolina collectively demonstrated. The researchers compared 138 studies that were designed to test progress monitoring or streaking and its influence on goal achievement. The study of studies concluded that those who kept a streak counter were more likely to achieve goals such as losing weight, lowering blood pressure and quitting smoking.

The same tool can also help you. But I've added an extra twist.

The major flaw of streaking is exposed when you stop. Seeing your counter rewind to zero hurts. You can't face the idea of starting over again, so you stop.

Here's the twist: you never stop streaking. You just count the blips.

Say your goal is to write a book and your daily step for the next 28 days is to write 250 words. Imagine you put a cross on your calendar for every day you bash those words out. Your motivation is sky high. Then suddenly on day 21 life trips you up and you don't write at all. The streak is over. Or is it?

It's a 28-day game

Blips are part of the learning process. Rather than panic and allow a slip to derail your motivational plan, mark down the blip and keep streaking. This "streaking with a twist" method becomes more about your 28-day total. Just imagine you get to the end of the 28 days and you have one or two blips. That's still a massive win, right?

This does not mean you have tactical days off. When you stumble it should hurt. The trick is to learn from this pain and come back stronger. The idea is to create the longest streak possible but, if you slip, to bounce back and keep streaking. Over time streaks will get longer until you become a blip-free zone.

Tracking less tangible goals

It's even more important to track goals that don't fit neatly into a box, such as "getting an amicable divorce" or "improving communication with your boss". For example, if your goal is to improve communication with your boss, the goal step could be one positive interaction with them per day. This interaction would be what you marked on your calendar. Each day you have a positive interaction, you mark with an 'X'. As the streak builds, so will your motivation, as you now have a physical sign that you're making progress.

Because these goals are less tangible, a streak counter can be extremely motivating. So aim to fit any goal into a daily streak counter and remember this twist.

Wednesday 3/4/2020

DAY I CHECK-IN

My goal is ..... *Learn to use my Q-20* .....

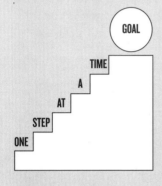

GOAL

TIME

A

AT

STEP

ONE

GOAL DATE

6/1/20

I. Morning power question
What can I do today to improve my motivational process? ....
....

2. Evening check-in
Did I do my best to [insert goal step] today? What did I do? ....
....

3. Streak checkbox

4. Score your positivity streams

#I Sleep	#2 Movement	#3 Nutrition	#4 Connection	#5 Quiet time	#6 Clear thinking
I	I	I	I	I	I
2	2	2	2	2	2
3	3	3	3	3	3
4	4	4	4	4	4
5	5	5	5	5	5
6	6	6	6	6	6
7	7	7	7	7	7
8	8	8	8	8	8
9	9	9	9	9	9
10	10	10	10	10	10

DAY 2: SET UP YOUR TRIGGER

Both your primitive and your human brain love habits, because they save precious energy. Once a habit is formed, your primitive brain runs it on autopilot. Part of your motivational mission over the next 28 days is to turn your goal step into a healthy habit. The quickest way to do this is to hijack an existing habit and use that as your new trigger.

Charles Duhigg, whom we met when we were looking at habits on page 85, brings the subconscious world of habits to life by demonstrating how they are formed when four elements come together to create a habit loop.

The habit loop: trigger > routine > reward > craving

- Trigger – there is a cue that starts the habit process
- Routine – the trigger kick-starts the habit routine
- Reward – at the end of the routine is the reward
- Craving – this drives the whole loop as you crave another reward

As long as there is a reward in the loop, your brain does not question the actions, it just gets on with it.

Identify your trigger

Over the next few weeks everything you will learn is designed to help you form a new healthy goal-step habit. For now let's play the habit game and get trigger happy.

Your trigger might be a time, action, preceding event or other people. Your world is already full of habits, from having a shower to kissing your partner when you arrive home. Today you're going to use an existing habit to kick-start your daily goal step.

Your goal step is the action you need to perform over and over in order to reach your goal. It doesn't have to be exactly the same every day – if your goal is, for example, starting a new part-time business, then you might research business ideas one day and develop your LinkedIn network the next. The thing that makes this a consistent habit is dedicating the time to step toward that goal. If you complete enough goal steps, you eventually reach the moonshot.

The classic habit trigger is your morning alarm. When it goes off, you press "play" on a host of habits to prepare for the day. This is a great place to hide a new goal step.

For example, could you use the daily habitual trigger of brushing your teeth to fire off your journaling routine, which can then trigger your movement goal step to go for a run, jump on a bike or do a quick HIIT session?

Think about lunch times, after work or when the kids are settled in bed. All of these little daily routines are already fully loaded with triggers and habits for you to hijack. Your mission is to find one that could also launch your goal step.

Add in a cheeky fist pump

B J Fogg is the director of the Stanford Behavior Design lab and a thought leader in behaviour change. He believes one of the most powerful things he has learned from all his years of study is that tiny habits can lead to massive change. He has even created a movement around showing people how to change their lives based on his Tiny Habits model. And one of the key elements to locking in a habit is to create a mini celebration.

So every time you finish your goal step, celebrate. I'm not talking

CASE STUDY:

CLAIRE DID IT

Claire was struggling to find consistency in her goal of finding a new job. She had a vague plan to spend 30 minutes per day researching new roles. But the days passed and her goal step was erratic at best.

So we worked on a plan and Claire decided to hijack her lunch break to trigger her daily job-search goal step. She did not have to create a new habit, she just had to leverage the power of the existing one. She no longer had to spend the day trying to find a random half hour. As she ate lunch, without thinking, Claire was triggered into pressing "play" on her goal step. Quickly she became consistent and found a new job. Sounds too easy, but this is the power of hijacking existing habits. They will help you to keep doing the things you need to do, in order to reach your goal.

about fireworks and party poppers, just a fist pump will do. Too cringeworthy? Don't knock it until you try it. Having a moment of celebration each time you complete a goal step provides a reward that signals to the brain to lock this goal into your subconscious.

But my goal requires more than one step per day

Great! Attach these steps to a series of existing triggers. For example, your goal might be to build your social media presence. Could you create an Insta story after you moisturize, comment on five other profiles while you're queuing for your coffee and use your commute home to prepare an evening post? You get the idea. It's the same hijacking process for each step.

Over time, you will associate your existing triggers with your new goal-step routine. So you won't have to think, "When should I run/write/paint?" – you will just feel the tug of your trigger and press "play" on your goal step.

Remember!

Winging it doesn't work. So having your goal step linked to an existing habit provides a clear signal to execute it. You cannot run from these triggers, so they will hold you accountable.

DAY 2 CHECK-IN

My goal is ....

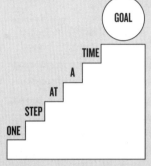

GOAL

TIME

A

AT

STEP

ONE

GOAL DATE

__/__/__

1. Morning power question

What can I do today to improve my motivational process? ....

....

2. Evening check-in

Did I do my best to [insert goal step] today? What did I do? ....

....

3. Streak checkbox ☐

4. Score your positivity streams

#1 Sleep	#2 Movement	#3 Nutrition	#4 Connection	#5 Quiet time	#6 Clear thinking
1	1	1	1	1	1
2	2	2	2	2	2
3	3	3	3	3	3
4	4	4	4	4	4
5	5	5	5	5	5
6	6	6	6	6	6
7	7	7	7	7	7
8	8	8	8	8	8
9	9	9	9	9	9
10	10	10	10	10	10

DAY 3: TAKE A TIME MACHINE

During a One Year No Beer podcast I did with Rosamund Dean, author of *Mindful Drinking*, she flippantly mentioned that we have roughly 4,000 weeks to live on this planet. My head was spinning: this couldn't be true. There was so much I wanted to do, how was I going to fit my dreams into a few weeks?

As soon as the interview was over, I did the math. To my horror, I only had 1,872 weeks left. Panic motivation ensued. I needed quick fixes and fast passes to my remaining goals and dreams. The more I felt time poor, the faster I wanted solutions and the less motivated I felt.

The conventional thinking is to motivate ourselves by connecting with how little time we have. Until recently I was guilty of this approach until I realized it didn't work. The truth is that you *do* have enough time to find the motivation to do anything you want. It just takes a plan and commitment.

Eventually when the time-is-short motivation spark wore off, I made another discovery about time that was to change everything.

Let's do the time-warp

In life you get what you focus on. A fixation on retirement age, a number made up by the government, can put a lid on your life. There is an underlying assumption that once you reach your 60s you stop contributing. What a load of rubbish.

Retirement thinking trips us up in two ways. Firstly, anyone approaching the made-up retirement age, often starts to believe it's too late to change. I continually hear 30- and 40-year-olds telling me how they are too old to change career, create a business or start a new hobby. It makes me want to yell.

Some brilliant research from Anders Ericsson, professor of psychology at Florida State University, suggests that it takes 10 years or 10,000 hours of deliberate practice to become, not just proficient, but a master of your craft or a virtuoso. Bill Gates offered more timely wisdom when he said, "We always overestimate the change that will occur in the next two years and underestimate the change that will occur in the next ten. Don't let yourself be lulled into inaction."

What Gates and Ericsson are both telling us is that it's never too late to be great. If you are anything like me, I am sure you have every intention of remaining mentally and physically active into your 80s and beyond. So why let retirement age put a limit on your contribution to the world? Let's *not* do this!

Forget retirement age. Let's look at this time thing all differently.

Take out your journal and let's do the time-warp. I'll do it with you...

Step 1: Write down your age. **44**

Step 2: Note down the age you believe you
will still be contributing to life. **90**

Step 3: Finally, subtract your current
age from your contribution age. **90 – 44 = 46 years**

Do the math and tell me you don't have the time to transform your body, change career or learn the guitar?

Not only do you have the time, but you could, in theory, be world class and a master of many crafts. In my example, I could be a virtuoso in four more disciplines before I reach 90 and, guess what? If I am feeling good at 90 I reckon I could master something else before I reach the big 100!

Fauja Singh took up running in his 80s after moving from Punjab to London. Nicknamed "The Turbaned Tornado", he ran the 2011 Toronto marathon in eight hours, eleven minutes. Fauja was 100 years old. There is always time.

Forget the shortness of life. It's long enough; we just need to know how to use it. And let's drop retirement as a marker that suggests we no longer contribute. This is when we start. We are all just warming up.

DAY 3 CHECK-IN

My goal is ....

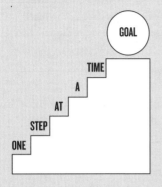

GOAL

TIME

A

AT

STEP

ONE

GOAL DATE

__ / __ / __

I. Morning power question
What can I do today to improve my motivational process? ....
....

2. Evening check-in
Did I do my best to [insert goal step] today? What did I do? ....
....

3. Streak checkbox ☐

4. Score your positivity streams

#I Sleep	#2 Movement	#3 Nutrition	#4 Connection	#5 Quiet time	#6 Clear thinking
I	I	I	I	I	I
2	2	2	2	2	2
3	3	3	3	3	3
4	4	4	4	4	4
5	5	5	5	5	5
6	6	6	6	6	6
7	7	7	7	7	7
8	8	8	8	8	8
9	9	9	9	9	9
I0	I0	I0	I0	I0	I0

DAY 4: MASTER YOUR MORNINGS

Early-morning goal routines are superpower motivators for two reasons. First, your willpower tanks are full and second, it's much harder for life to get in the way of a morning goal step. But if you really can't find time in the morning, you can find it later in the day. You always have more time than you realize.

Having left school at 16 to chase the dream of becoming a footballer, I left the dream of higher education behind. In my early 30s, while I was working in London as a broker, that dream resurfaced. I kept telling people, usually over a few beers, how I was going to study part-time. They would smile and order another round. But I couldn't find the time or energy to do anything about it. In my mind there was no time outside work, family, stress, repeat. My life was more about staying afloat than gaining degrees.

Then a friend suggested getting up earlier. I laughed. In my mind this was one of those chocolate-teapot pieces of wisdom. Useless. There was no time in the morning. There was no time anywhere. I had a family and a mega-busy job and social life. And every day was a fight with the alarm. I dismissed my mate's idea immediately.

What's funny is that back then, before I figured out that motivation is a skill, I couldn't comprehend how I could find more time. So I totally understand if you feel the same. But my friend's comments stuck with me, so a few months later I thought I would give the early mornings a try. Straight away I made the schoolboy error of assuming I could jump up at 5am fresh as a daisy. I was wrong. After a few days of not enough sleep the 5am dream was producing diminishing returns.

So I gave up. Until two years later, when I read *The Miracle Morning* by Hal Elrod and discovered the most obvious truth. You cannot beat the sandman. If you need seven and a half hours (five sleep cycles), then that's what you need. My first attempt did not take this into account. So now it was clear. If I wanted to get up earlier, I would have to go to sleep earlier. But I didn't have time. Or did I?

Find that time

Start to look at your life through the lens of someone who wants to maximize every second. What are the things, people, jobs, tasks, commitments that take up a lot of time but offer little in return? What can you take away to give time back?

For me, it started with TV. My wife Tara and I had formed a habit of watching box sets (this was before Netflix) from 9pm to 11pm, after the kids were settled. In our minds this was our quality time. But was it? We were exhausted and barely a word was spoken as we stayed up late, lifelessly watching the screen.

On reflection, this was not quality time. We were staying up in order to feel as if we had a life outside being parents, when actually we were too tired to enjoy those hours. And I certainly didn't have the energy to do anything meaningful with the time.

So I suggested we go to sleep earlier, wake earlier and grab some quality time in the morning. It worked. We started going to bed at 10pm to get up for 5.30am and then pushed that back to 9.30pm to wake up at a miraculous 5am. This was a total game changer.

I now had two hours before work and before the kids were awake. You can change the world in two hours a day. Just imagine what you could achieve in this time slot. It was during this time that I studied, wrote my first book and co-founded the One Year No Beer movement. But I realize that getting up at 5am won't work for everyone. It just worked for me. It's finding the time to perform your goal step that matters.

Can you find 15, 30 or even 60 minutes before your day begins to execute your goal step?

Think like a motivational pro

If your absolute dream is to quit the office job to become a psychologist but you can't find time to study, think again. Before you write off your dreams, work through the six streams of positivity to ensure by operating at peak vitality you find the time you need. If you reduce your alcohol intake, improve your sleep, eat well and move more you will find hidden pockets of time. Fact.

I know that for some people mornings are genuinely impossible, but can you find time at lunchtime or in the evening? If you're a night owl, arrange your goal steps for later in the day when the world is slowing down. Be a hunter of quality time and remember what the Roman philosopher Seneca said 2,000 years ago: "It's not that we don't have enough time, it's just that we waste so much of it."

DAY4 CHECK-IN

My goal is...

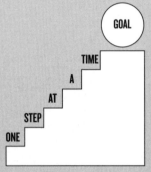

GOAL

TIME

A

AT

STEP

ONE

GOAL DATE

__/__/__

I. Morning power question

What can I do today to improve my motivational process?...

....

2. Evening check-in

Did I do my best to [insert goal step] today? What did I do?...

....

3. Streak checkbox

4. Score your positivity streams

#I Sleep	#2 Movement	#3 Nutrition	#4 Connection	#5 Quiet time	#6 Clear thinking
I	I	I	I	I	I
2	2	2	2	2	2
3	3	3	3	3	3
4	4	4	4	4	4
5	5	5	5	5	5
6	6	6	6	6	6
7	7	7	7	7	7
8	8	8	8	8	8
9	9	9	9	9	9
I0	I0	I0	I0	I0	I0

DAY 5: FIND OUT WHO YOU REALLY ARE

Today let's jump straight into the exercise – we can chat afterward. Find a quiet space and open up your journal.

Now come along with me as we drift into a gentle visualization.

I want you to imagine yourself a few years from now. Having read this book and mastered your own motivation, you're crushing your goals and loving life in the process. While travelling, you bump into an old friend. After catching up for a while your friend continues to articulate how great you're looking and is truly in awe of the things you have achieved. But they are finding life tough. They don't seem to have enough time in the day. Their life is: stress; family; work; repeat. They are lost and struggling to find any meaning or purpose. Suddenly, your friend notices the clock and has to run to catch a train. But before they go, they ask: "Please help, and give me your best advice. How should I live my life?"

Your friend has put you on the spot. But you can't freeze, you have to connect with your deep values and inner wisdom to help guide them. And remember, you have to sum up these ideas quickly before your friend runs for their train.

Take 60 seconds to answer their question; see what comes up and write it down. Don't overthink it; just let the words flow onto the paper.

When you have finished, read on.

This visualization is a stealth way to connect with the important things in your life. The time pressure stops you overthinking it. And what bubbles up first is often the most precious to you.

Now, I want to challenge you: are you living by the wonderful wisdom you just gifted your friend?

What this visualization really does is help you unlock the things that are most dear to you. If you're willing to give this beautiful advice to someone else, then surely it makes sense that you also live by these ideas?

The trick to this exercise is that you're not really giving your wisdom away. You're giving power advice to yourself.

Now I want you to take this advice and put it into a personal authentic-self manifesto. Write it down. It might be a page long, a paragraph or just a sentence. Do it now. When you're ready, read on.

This exercise is so important for igniting your motivation, because when your goals are aligned with your authentic-self manifesto, lasting motivation is yours. When we are aligned with who we really are, we become unstoppable. The authentic-self manifesto is the start of your personal mission to reconnect with you. Because we forget who we really are so quickly. Life and stress want to push us around and we lose touch with our true sense of self.

But you're different now. You are taking back control and, from now on, I want you to reconnect with your authentic-self every. single. day.

CASE STUDY:

Here are a few authentic-self manifestos from students who have taken my masterclass. There are no rights or wrongs. The key, as always, is that you connect with this on a daily basis.

RAE

Be kind: to yourself. To others.

Value yourself, value connections, value loving relationships, value the earth and its resources, value achievement and value the things you own. Anything you value has taken work to create, so do not dismiss or rubbish it and don't be wasteful.

Don't let others dictate your values. They are yours.

Use your hands, move your body and sing at the top of your lungs.

Always look out for others. Be the ear and be the cheer. But look out for yourself too.

Learn to make the most of fear and anxiety. They can save or destroy you.

Most of all, travel, listen, talk and love.

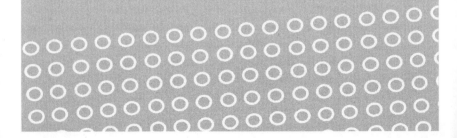

EMMA

Be kind to other people, to animals and plants, to our planet and most importantly to yourself.

Seek out connections — love, friendship, shared dreams or visions — don't be alone.

Get out there — connect, travel, experience, enjoy, be amazed.

Be open to new things always — ideas, experiences, places, people, smells and flavours of life.

Don't waste time on anger, jealousy or regrets — do stuff that makes you happy, and relish the time spent doing it.

Embrace who you are, the way that you are, whatever that is, and own it.

Smile.

ANDY (YES, ME. I WRITE THIS AUTHENTIC-SELF STATEMENT EVERY DAY)

Be a hero

Be a leader

B A Baracus (it's almost impossible not to put Baracus after those B A's)

Be grateful

Be kind

Be generous

Be loved and love

Be mindful

Be an athlete

Be afraid and love it

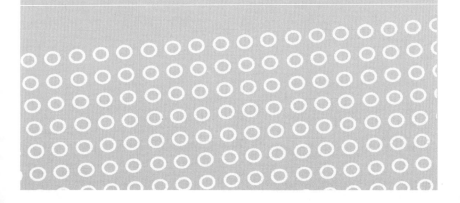

Keep refining

If you notice ideas within your authentic-self manifesto that you are not currently aligned to, then use this as fuel for future goals.

For example, you might have written "Travel the world." However, travelling is not currently on your radar. Perhaps it sounds nice, but it is not something you're actively embracing. Ask yourself, is this really what I want to focus on? If it is, then use your motivational mastery to introduce more travel into your world. If it's not, perhaps consider removing this idea from your authentic-self manifesto. You might find that you're saying what you think people want you to say. But honestly, what do you really want?

Likewise, if there are ideas that you aspire to, such as to "show more courage", then include these in your authentic-self manifesto and start working toward them.

Finally, put your manifesto somewhere you can see it on a daily basis. You could write it in the front of your journal, put a Post-it note on your PC, write it on the kitchen blackboard or create a framed copy to hang on the bathroom wall. I have seen all these examples and more, but whatever you decide, put it somewhere that you can see it every day.

The aim of today's class is to reconnect you with who you really are, to identify where you are going and most importantly how you are going to get there.

DAY 5 CHECK-IN

My goal is ....

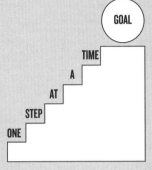

GOAL

TIME

A

AT

STEP

ONE

GOAL DATE

__/__/__

1. Morning power question
What can I do today to improve my motivational process? ....

....

2. Evening check-in
Did I do my best to [insert goal step] today? What did I do? ....

....

3. Streak checkbox

4. Score your positivity streams

#1 Sleep	#2 Movement	#3 Nutrition	#4 Connection	#5 Quiet time	#6 Clear thinking
1	1	1	1	1	1
2	2	2	2	2	2
3	3	3	3	3	3
4	4	4	4	4	4
5	5	5	5	5	5
6	6	6	6	6	6
7	7	7	7	7	7
8	8	8	8	8	8
9	9	9	9	9	9
10	10	10	10	10	10

DAY 6: BUILD YOUR DREAM BOAT CREW

Jim Rohn, a motivational guru, was famous for saying, "You're the average of the five people you spend the most time with." He was right, but it's not just your five friends, but their friends and *their* friends who influence your motivation.

Network researcher Nicholas Christakis, whom in 2009 *TIME* magazine listed as one of the hundred most influential people in the world, revealed how our social networks influence behaviour. Christakis and his team were fascinated by the idea of obesity infecting the United States like a plague. It was clear obesity was rising but, Christakis wanted to know, was it spreading from person to person?

By fluke a heart study provided the data he needed. The now famous Framingham Heart Study collected data from hundreds of thousands of people in Framingham, Massachusetts, from 1948 to 2000, about their weight, moods, habits and most importantly their connections.

Christakis and his team spent years combing the data and building all the interconnected networks between family, friends and their friends. Finally Christakis confirmed that our actions, good and bad, flow within our network. Nothing too exciting there.

But what he did not expect was just how *far* habits and emotions could spread. According to Christakis's research, if your friend becomes obese your chances of joining them jumps by 45 per cent.

Then it gets crazy: if one of your friend's friends becomes overweight, your chances of piling on the pounds still goes up 25 per cent.

There's more. If your friend's friend's friend puts on weight, you are 10 per cent more likely to see your waistline increase. How mind-blowing is this?

Remember
If you don't have a plan, your friends have a plan for you. And so do their friends and *their* friends.

How to build your dream boat crew

There will be people in your life who support your dreams and those who don't. What Christakis demonstrated is that both influence your motivation. I will go a step further and suggest that the books you read, podcasts you listen to and TV or videos you watch also hinder or help motivate you. So assemble a dream boat crew who will cheer you on and also inspire you to greatness.

Step 1 – Spend more time with the cheerleaders

Be deliberate about who you spend your time with and build this into your motivational plan. You know the people who will motivate you from the sidelines and those who won't. Think tactical. Perhaps use this idea as a chance to improve your "connection" positivity stream score and create a win-win.

Your primitive brain loves to know who's part of your support crew. This comes from a powerful instinctual drive to stay part of the group. Because back in the days when we roamed the savannah, being thrown out of the tribe meant death. This is why we bend so easily to social pressure and why tribes can be fantastic motivational tools, as you will discover on day 13.

So I would like you to take out your journal and draw a boat like the one below:

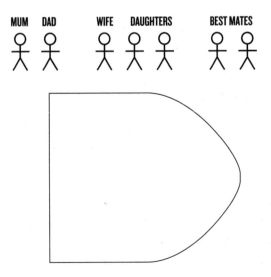

BECAUSE BACK IN THE DAYS WHEN
WE ROAMED THE SAVANNAH,
BEING THROWN OUT OF THE TRIBE
MEANT DEATH

Now list all the people you would want to see cheering you on. It's probably a small group: think family and very close friends.

This will help your motivation in two ways. First, you will know exactly who your support crew are, and therefore who's opinions matter. Second, as Christakis shows us, the positive motivational vibes from your support crew will influence your motivation.

Step 2 – Set up your dream boat crew

Imagine you could ask anyone in the world, past and present, to form part of your dream boat – who would you choose? Think about people who have already achieved your dream. Can you find their biographies, TED talks or blog posts that will fill you with their wisdom to make your boat go faster?

What about inspirational characters or coaches? If you put them in the boat, how could they help you? What could you learn from them?

You can also guarantee there is someone out there just like you, an everyday hero, who has achieved what it is you are trying to accomplish. They might be a friend, family member, colleague or boss. Go find them, learn from them and add them to your dream boat.

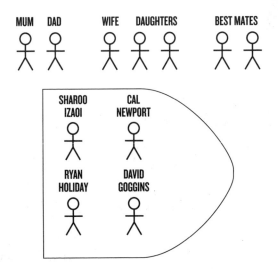

Here's my dream boat crew for my goal of writing this book

All of my dream boat crew are authors, influencers and great motivators:

- **Cal Newport** – his concept of deep work (see page 56) helped me find the dedicated time to do the study and write this book
- **David Goggins** – reading and listening to his stuff is motivational rocket fuel
- **Shahroo Izadi** – my good pal reminds me that my writing will suck at times, but with kindness I can keep learning and getting better
- **Ryan Holiday** – when it comes to writing, Ryan is the guy I learn from. His book on writing, *Perennial Seller*, is gold dust

What now?

Once you have your cheerleaders and crew assembled, spend as much time as you can with the cheerleaders and devour everything you can from your dream boat crew.

Finally, if it holds that we're motivated by our connections, then we can influence the people closest to us. Therefore, and this is where it gets exciting, our motivation can motivate the people we love. Doesn't that motivate you more?

DAY 6 CHECK-IN

My goal is ....

GOAL

TIME
A
AT
STEP
ONE

GOAL DATE

__/__/__

1. Morning power question

What can I do today to improve my motivational process? ....

....

2. Evening check-in

Did I do my best to [insert goal step] today? What did I do? ....

....

3. Streak checkbox

4. Score your positivity streams

#1 Sleep	#2 Movement	#3 Nutrition	#4 Connection	#5 Quiet time	#6 Clear thinking
1	1	1	1	1	1
2	2	2	2	2	2
3	3	3	3	3	3
4	4	4	4	4	4
5	5	5	5	5	5
6	6	6	6	6	6
7	7	7	7	7	7
8	8	8	8	8	8
9	9	9	9	9	9
10	10	10	10	10	10

DAY 7: REFRAME SUCCESS

When you set out on your motivational adventure, it's natural to expect you'll be perfect. But life is not perfect, so mistakes happen. Redefining what success means during your quest can boost motivation and keep you on track to reach your goals.

The traditional perfection mindset leaves no room for error. Your primitive brain views setbacks or a perceived lack of progress as reasons to give up. Whereas redefining success creates space for progress, even if you stumble.

Try a percentage improvement approach

For example, instead of viewing junk food as an all-or-nothing abstinence competition, set yourself a percentage reduction.

Redefining success in terms of a percentage reduction leaves room for an unexpected fumble. If you have been eating junk food daily and, during your 28-day masterclass, you only slip up twice, that is still a 93 per cent reduction in junk-food consumption. That's pretty good, right? And your primitive brain likes it when you're doing well. This will fuel motivation to keep going, growing stronger, and maybe during the following 28 days there will be no slips.

You can redefine success with any goal. Rather than that bargain shirt causing a sense of doom, you might connect with the days when you did stick to your savings plan and acknowledge the percentage improvement. Also don't forget that, as we saw on day 1, streaking with a twist will help create a visual representation of how much you're improving.

So if you want to write a book but miss a few days at your laptop, dust yourself off and keep going until the end of the month, then review your percentage progress versus last month.

By moving away from a perfection mindset, we create space to view any slip as a one-off that has something to teach us. One indiscretion does not need to impact the overall objective. And as you will discover on day 12, failure is baked into the change process: the stumbling stones are there to teach us how to be better next time, not a reason to give up.

DAY 7 CHECK-IN

My goal is ....

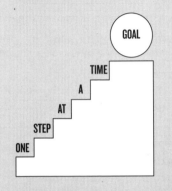

GOAL

TIME

A

AT

STEP

ONE

GOAL DATE

__/__/__

1. Morning power question

What can I do today to improve my motivational process? ....
....

2. Evening check-in

Did I do my best to [insert goal step] today? What did I do? ....
....

3. Streak checkbox

4. Score your positivity streams

#1 Sleep	#2 Movement	#3 Nutrition	#4 Connection	#5 Quiet time	#6 Clear thinking
1	1	1	1	1	1
2	2	2	2	2	2
3	3	3	3	3	3
4	4	4	4	4	4
5	5	5	5	5	5
6	6	6	6	6	6
7	7	7	7	7	7
8	8	8	8	8	8
9	9	9	9	9	9
10	10	10	10	10	10

What you learned this week

Day 1 – Start streaking with a twist: track your days and, if you blip, learn and keep moving

Day 2 – Hijack your trigger: use existing habits to fire off your new goal steps

Day 3 – The time machine: you do have time; remember you're just warming up

Day 4 – Mornings are golden: unlock even more time before the world is awake

Day 5 – Authentic-self manifesto: align with who you really are to unlock motivation

Day 6 – Dream boat: create your support crew and dream boat for extra inspiration and motivation

Day 7 – Reframe success: it's not about being perfect, it's about learning and growing

See how far you've come

Hopefully you can feel the motivational empowerment flowing through your body. The key to this whole process is that you take the framework I am showing you and then own it. Do not let anyone – or yourself, for that matter – tell you that you don't have the motivation to achieve your dreams, because you do. Much of this book is dedicated to removing those well-worn excuses we have all used in the past, such as "I don't have enough time", "I can't do it because I am not good or clever enough" and the big one – "I don't have the motivation". Because once these excuses are gone and you discover who you really are, you become unstoppable.

I know it's scary when you realize that you and you alone are responsible for your dreams, because it leaves nowhere to hide. But this forces you, in the most positive way, to take control of your destiny, and this is where the magic of life resides. So use the rituals, the accountability centre, and let's make things happen. All I ask is that you keep showing up for the rest of this book and experience the whole 28-day process for yourself. Then, when you finish, think about the time-machine exercise we did on day 3 and remember you are just warming up.

Week 2 – Overcome Resistance

Right now, not everyone is behind your goal. And the most dangerous enemy of all comes from within – you know, that voice that says, "I can't."

Actually, you can.

This week, we're going to take on resistance in all its different forms. Day by day, you'll deal with your detractors and seek out your supporters. You'll learn the art of being kind to yourself, show your inner saboteur who's boss, train your inner cheerleader and find a tribe to cheer you on. Falling in love with failure is also an important lesson, and the one that will power you through the rollercoaster ride to smashing your goal.

Let's do this.

DAY 8: BE KIND TO YOURSELF

Procrastination and inaction tempt us to bring out the stick of guilt, to beat ourselves with words such as "You're lazy", "You have no motivation" or "Everyone else can do it." This is the conventional approach to motivation. You hit yourself with a big enough stick in the hope it will get you moving.

Perhaps this approach has appeared to work in the past – for a short time. But what eventually happens is that the sticks of guilt and shame hurt so much that we hide from them. And the best way to avoid the pain is to quit our goal and jump back into the comfort zone where it's safe and we don't have to take action or fail.

Once again this motivational wisdom is wrong. Kindness and compassion are rocket fuel to motivation.

Why kindness works

After ten years of battling with her body, Shahroo Izadi, author of *The Kindness Method*, lost almost 51kg (112lb) – that's eight stone! – because she had finally broken the stick of guilt. How? She found lasting motivation in self-compassion. Shahroo and I became good friends after we met at a book launch. When I asked her how she had found the motivation to transform her body and life, she summed it up beautifully: "It was self-compassion and kindness that gave me the space to stop hiding from my goals and start taking action."

Pause for a moment and take in the fact that Shahroo, like you and me, was not born with cast-iron willpower. She isn't perfect. She had to work hard to master her motivation, but once she did she improved her life beyond measure.

Shahroo's story shows us that, when you approach life with self-compassion, you're able to appreciate that you're only human. We've all procrastinated, we've all failed to take action and we all make mistakes. The thing that makes some people exceptional is that they build self-compassion into their plan.

Why does it work? Some brilliant research from the Carleton University in Ottawa, Canada, kept a record of how often students procrastinated during a term. The team also tracked how the students tried to motivate themselves. Those who used the traditional method of the stick and who berated themselves for not studying were even more likely to procrastinate on the subsequent exams. And the harder they were on themselves, the more they procrastinated. The conclusion is that guilt makes us want to hide and distance ourselves from our actions. So we miss the opportunity to learn and we make more mistakes, whereas taking personal responsibility for inaction or failures allowed the students to learn and adapt, so they were better prepared to study for the following exam. Or, in other words, self-compassion and not the stick of guilt helped motivate the students to study.

What's more, you will also feel happier if you are compassionate to yourself, as you don't have to beat yourself up verbally. This does not mean you're soft. It doesn't mean you can let yourself off the hook. Self-compassion is a courageous act, being strong enough to say, "I am going to own my life, warts and all." In doing so you create the perfect environment to grow lasting motivation. And remember, you are a perfectly imperfect human.

Unleash your self-compassion in five minutes

This is not a fluffy exercise. But it is called Loving Kindness Meditation, so bear with me. LKM is an unbelievably powerful gateway to self-compassion. And it comes with a warning. After you have performed the meditation below you will be filled with compassion and kindness and might want to hug everyone you see today, from the delivery guy to that jerk who barged in front of you in the supermarket.

You don't need to know anything about meditation, or to sit cross-legged on a cloud. All you need to do is follow the steps below.

Step 1 – Find a quiet space and get comfortable
Set a timer for five minutes. Close your eyes. Inhale and exhale deeply three times.

Step 2 – Focus on someone you love
Once you're settled, recite the following mantra over and over in your head. Say a line very slowly as you breathe in and then the next line as you breathe out.

YOU WILL BE FILLED WITH
COMPASSION AND KINDNESS
AND MIGHT WANT TO HUG
EVERYONE YOU SEE TODAY

In breath: May [xxx] be happy
Out breath: May [xxx] be healthy
In breath: May [xxx] be loved

The idea is that you start with the name of the person closest to you and then expand your awareness to other close family and friends. As you cycle through each of their names, imagine them in your mind's eye. Fill up your chest and heart with love and compassion as you do so.

Step 3 – Open your reach

Now expand your reach to include groups of people: all your friends, your wider family, colleagues and other connections. Use the same method as in step 2.

In breath: May [all my friends] be happy
Out breath: May [all my friends] be healthy
In breath: May [all my friends] be loved

Step 4 – Include yourself

Some people find this step the hardest. But now you are in the loving groove, put yourself into the mantra and immerse yourself in self-compassion. This is where the power lies.

In breath: May I be happy
Out breath: May I be healthy
In breath: May I be loved

Step 5 – Take on the world

This is my favourite part of the meditation. Once you're on a roll, include your whole local area, then your city, your country and finally the world. Build this up to a crescendo of compassion. Feel it bursting out of your chest as the love pours out into the planet. Stay with these feelings and gently come back to earth.

When you feel ready, open your eyes, with a massive smile. Feel the self-compassion, wallow in the love and keep an eye out for the delivery guy.

DAY 8 CHECK-IN

My goal is ....

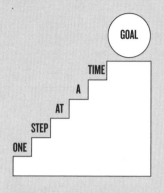

GOAL DATE

__/__/__

1. Morning power question
What can I do today to improve my motivational process? ....
....

2. Evening check-in
Did I do my best to [insert goal step] today? What did I do? ....
....

3. Streak checkbox

4. Score your positivity streams

#1 Sleep	#2 Movement	#3 Nutrition	#4 Connection	#5 Quiet time	#6 Clear thinking
1	1	1	1	1	1
2	2	2	2	2	2
3	3	3	3	3	3
4	4	4	4	4	4
5	5	5	5	5	5
6	6	6	6	6	6
7	7	7	7	7	7
8	8	8	8	8	8
9	9	9	9	9	9
10	10	10	10	10	10

DAY 9: SEE OFF YOUR SABOTEUR

Whenever your mind is tormented by something you want but at the same time don't want, you will find the subconscious saboteur.

The subconscious saboteur lives in your brain and creates ambivalence about your goal, which is when you have conflicting thoughts about the topic in question. Where there is ambivalence you need willpower to overcome it and we know that running goals on willpower doesn't work. So, if left unmanaged, the subconscious saboteur will continue to trip you up.

The subconscious saboteur can show up within any goal:

- I hate hangovers, but I love my wine
- I know how good eating healthily is, but I would love a kebab
- If I go for a run, I will feel great, but it's so cosy here on the couch
- I want to settle this divorce amicably, but I just want to yell at my ex

The ambivalence seesaw exercise

Your mission is to put the subconscious saboteur back in its box by breaking down any ambivalence you feel toward your goal. This works in two ways:

- First, you can dominate with the good stuff and drown out the ambivalence with all the positives about your goal. This might not make the ambivalence vanish, but the positives of sticking to your goal will outweigh it.
- Second, you can destroy the subconscious saboteur's power by proving that the positives of not sticking to your goal are actually negatives. For example, yelling at your ex will only end up making you feel worse.

Try the ambivalence seesaw exercise here to help see off the subconscious saboteur.

Step 1 – Draw the seesaw

In your journal, draw a seesaw and on the left write all the positives about your chosen goal. On the right list any perceived positives you still have about *not* performing the steps required to achieve your goal.

Mary's goal was to get a promotion at work. Her ambivalence seesaw looked like this:

POSITIVES OF GETTING A PROMOTION	PERCEIVED POSITIVES OF NOT GETTING A PROMOTION
Higher salary	Won't have to sit in endless meetings
More holidays	Fewer people to manage and worry about
Extra responsibility	Won't have to report to Mike
Potential stepping stone to directorship	I have it easy where I am so why rock the boat?

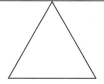

Step 2 – Stack the positives

Take a few minutes to load up the positive side of the seesaw (the list on the left-hand side). Write as many things as you can think of that might be classed as upsides to performing your goal steps. The idea is to keep adding to the left side so the list outweighs any perceived positives on the right.

For example, Mary went on to add:

POSITIVES OF GETTING A PROMOTION	PERCEIVED POSITIVES OF NOT GETTING A PROMOTION
More control over my actions	Won't have to sit in endless meetings
Chance to make a difference in way business is run	Fewer people to manage and worry about
Get to work with Claire whom I've always admired	Won't have to report to Mike
Might get a new desk	I have it easy where I am so why rock the boat?
Higher salary	
More holidays	
Extra responsibility	
Potential stepping stone to directorship	

Step 3 – Break down the ambivalence

The whole undercurrent of this exercise is to build up these positives, but the real power within it is to challenge the right-hand side of the seesaw and break down that ambivalence. First ask yourself – what is the belief pretending to offer? There must be some perceived upside. Then challenge this thinking.

Mary worked through each point of ambivalence until it lost its pulling power. For example, she hated meetings, which created ambivalence because if she did not get the promotion then she **"wouldn't have to sit in endless meetings"**. To help break this ambivalence down, I encouraged Mary to talk to a colleague who performed a similar role. This further investigation helped her discover that while she might have a few more meetings, she would also be in a position to control their duration. So "endless meetings" was a total overstatement; in truth she would be in control, which was a positive for promotion. Her **"won't have to sit in endless meetings"** ambivalence was losing its power.

She then moved on to the next ambivalence point, and the next, and treated them in the same way. When she came to **"I have it easy where I am, so why rock the boat?"**, on reflection she realized that this was her primitive brain speaking, attempting to keep her stuck in her comfort zone. She had to make peace with the fact that this promotion would be scary and would take her *outside* the comfort zone, but she now knew that that was where all the growth, learning and ultimately happiness resided. Her **"I have it easy where I am, so why rock the boat?"** was quashed.

Doing a little extra work can help reveal your subconscious saboteur and you can then find ways to overcome it. This is the beauty of checking in with your goal and your goal steps each day, as it brings a mindful awareness to moments of ambivalence, which is just another tactic that your primitive brain uses to continue the status quo.

DAY 9 CHECK-IN

My goal is ....
.

GOAL

TIME

A

AT

STEP

ONE

GOAL DATE

_ _ / _ _ / _ _

1. Morning power question

What can I do today to improve my motivational process? ....

....

2. Evening check-in

Did I do my best to [insert goal step] today? What did I do? ....

....

3. Streak checkbox

4. Score your positivity streams

#1 Sleep	#2 Movement	#3 Nutrition	#4 Connection	#5 Quiet time	#6 Clear thinking
1	1	1	1	1	1
2	2	2	2	2	2
3	3	3	3	3	3
4	4	4	4	4	4
5	5	5	5	5	5
6	6	6	6	6	6
7	7	7	7	7	7
8	8	8	8	8	8
9	9	9	9	9	9
10	10	10	10	10	10

DAY 10: GO GREEN

Over 2,000 years ago the Roman nobleman Cornelius Celsus wrote an encyclopedia that contained a section – De Medicina – considered the greatest account of Roman medicine. Within these pages, Celsus described how walking in nature, exposure to natural light and being close to water were effective treatments to improve mental health and sleep. Practitioners within Chinese medicine and the Indian Ayurveda tradition have for centuries promoted nature as a way to heal the mind and body. More recently, in the early 1900s nature retreats were prescribed as a tonic to the increasing complexity of the industrialized world. But as the 1900s progressed, nature as a cure lost scientific support. Slowly nature was pushed out of traditional medicine into pseudoscience where it remained along with baldness cures until a Japanese marketing campaign changed everything.

In 1982 Tomohide Akiyama, director of Japan's forest agency, hatched a plan to inspire the populace back into nature by "shinrin-yoku", which loosely translates as forest-bathing. What started out as a drive to help the Japanese benefit from those instinctive pleasures of green spaces, such as peace, awe and happiness, eventually resulted in a flood of scientific studies. This new wave of nature-based science confirmed what Cornelius and the healing traditions had always known: "shinrin-yoku", or forest-bathing, can reduce psychological stress, help with depression, improve sleep, enhance our cognitive abilities and, most importantly, increase vigour, energy and motivation.

Go green and power up your motivation

Getting outside into nature is the perfect way to de-stress, find quiet time, treat yourself kindly and unlock a new level of motivation.

Having worked in London for many years I had no idea how many parks and green spaces there were. I would continually rush past these green motivators because I was too busy doing "important stuff". But once I realized the power of greenery and slowed down, I began to notice lots of small parks and green spaces even in the City of London. I was astounded to discover that 47 per cent of London is green space and it's home to 8 million trees, making it one of the world's largest urban forests. So no matter where you're based, you will be able to find 5 to 10 minutes of green time and use its motivational power to help you reach your dreams.

How to unearth more green motivation

If you can't get outside to take a green shower (see opposite page), find a window with a view of nature, slow down and wallow in its glow. Brain imaging techniques have revealed that even looking at pictures of nature can activate the areas of the brain associated with happiness and positive emotions.

Another win-win is to take your movement routines outside. Could you run or walk 5k around the local park rather than on a treadmill? Research has shown that participants who took a one-hour nature-based walk improved their mental outlook and were more cognitively replenished than participants who walked in an urban setting.

House plants are like mini-motivators. Some great science shows that plants can reduce anxiety, lower blood pressure, reduce pain, as well as increase positive thoughts and energy.

While I totally appreciate our lives have changed so much over the last 70 years and nature is no longer a key ingredient of daily living, there are green spaces all around us. With a little creativity, you can quickly unlock the motivational power of nature on a daily basis.

Take a power green-shower

This exercise will make a big difference to your motivation and wellbeing. All you have to do is find a green space and be in it:

- Lunch breaks are the perfect time to go green.

- Can you find a small park or tree surrounded by some green perhaps with a park bench? Or is there a lawn near your office or even a rooftop garden? Or can you simply sit in your own garden at home with a cup of tea?

- Today, scan your local area at lunchtime for your green oasis.

- When your eyes are open to nature, you will start to notice more and more opportunities to go green.

- Once you have located your green space, all you have to do is sit or slowly walk for 5 minutes or more.

- Turn off the phone, breathe, slow down, smile and relax.

- That's it.

- After your green shower, when you've give your over-stimulated brain a little rest, you will feel more relaxed, yet invigorated and motivated.

DAY 10 CHECK-IN

My goal is ....

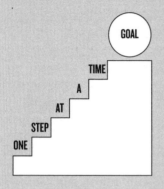

GOAL

TIME

A

AT

STEP

ONE

GOAL DATE

__ / __ / __

1. Morning power question

What can I do today to improve my motivational process? ....

....

2. Evening check-in

Did I do my best to [insert goal step] today? What did I do? ....

....

3. Streak checkbox ☐

4. Score your positivity streams

#1 Sleep	#2 Movement	#3 Nutrition	#4 Connection	#5 Quiet time	#6 Clear thinking
1	1	1	1	1	1
2	2	2	2	2	2
3	3	3	3	3	3
4	4	4	4	4	4
5	5	5	5	5	5
6	6	6	6	6	6
7	7	7	7	7	7
8	8	8	8	8	8
9	9	9	9	9	9
10	10	10	10	10	10

DAY 11: TRAIN YOUR INNER CHEERLEADER

Dr Steve Peters, the genius psychiatrist behind many elite athletes, says in his book *The Chimp Paradox* that your primitive brain can be your worst critic or your biggest fan. This is so true.

The biggest barrier to your goals is not ability, time or IQ: it's your own negative inner dialogue. Equally, as Dr Peters points out, when your inner primitive voice is aligned with your goal, it can become your greatest supporter.

Today your mission is to clean up your inner chatter, using the four-step process below, so the voices inside your head cheer you on rather than hold you back.

Step 1 – Uncover the demotivator

For the rest of today, I want you to listen out for your primitive brain talking. Write down in your journal what it says.

The primitive brain uses emotional and often critical language, for example:

- "You're lazy; you don't have time; what's the point in trying?"
- "You always give up"

Just getting this demotivating voice out of your head onto paper will instantly make a difference as you begin to notice that much of what's said inside your mind is total nonsense.

Once you have a few examples of your internal negative chatter the objective is to turn this demotivator into a cheerleader by applying the following steps

Step 2 – Skilfully detach yourself from the negative noise

The skill of mindfulness gives you the ability to allow your thoughts to pass through your mind without chasing every thought back into the past or into the future. The process of letting your thoughts go, reveals the great mindfulness secret – that you are not the thoughts in your head. Most of what's said internally is total nonsense so you don't have to believe the thoughts that appear in your mind.

If you can imagine your thoughts are like boats on a river. Mindfulness helps you to sit peacefully on the riverbank and watch each boat as it drifts past. There is no need to try and analyse each boat, it's just a boat gently moving downstream.

Therefore mindfulness can help you to distance yourself from the demotivating voices and act as your first motivational filter. Check out page 72 for a quick meditation.

Step 3 – Challenge your inner critic

Unfortunately, life is not all zen and no matter how mindful you are, there will be many times when you get sucked into the demotivating internal chatter. When this happens you can set up the next filter which is to challenge your inner critic.

The misconception that our internal language is the truth continually prevents us from achieving our goals. To help make this distinction I would like you to challenge the statements you noted down in step one when listening for your demotivator. The quickest way to do this is to form a counter-argument for each statement. For example:

- "You always give up"
- **Counter argument:** Has there ever been a time when you didn't "give up"?

The trick is to list as many examples of you not giving up as you possibly can. This filter demonstrates that the statement *"You always give up"* is totally untrue and just noise.

- I didn't give up when I ran the 10k last year"
- I didn't give up when my partner left and I had to raise the kids"
- I didn't give up on that promotion at work

Perform this counter-argument exercise with each statement. If it helps, imagine you're defending a friend – how many counter-examples can you create to disprove the demotivator?

Step 4 – Create a new empowering statement

With the demotivator on the ropes, your final mission is to turn it into a cheerleader. The best way to achieve this is to feed it a new empowering story.

Sticking to the example above, *"You always give up"*

Flip the demotivating language into an empowering statement.

"There have been many occasions in the past when I have persevered, even when I wanted to give up, and although this is hard I will continue to show up and do my best."

This whole process might feel a bit clunky at first. But over time the 4 step process will happen at lightning speed. To the point that any demotivating language you encounter that gets through the mindfulness step two, will be challenged with counter-arguments in step three and then flipped into the positive in step four.

What's even more impressive is that over time this will happen at a subconscious level and those former negative, horrible thoughts will be replaced with empowering ones. I cannot overstate how powerful this is.

DAY II CHECK-IN

My goal is...
.

GOAL

TIME
A
AT
STEP
ONE

GOAL DATE

__/__/__

I. Morning power question

What can I do today to improve my motivational process?...

....

2. Evening check-in

Did I do my best to [insert goal step] today? What did I do?...

....

3. Streak checkbox

4. Score your positivity streams

#I Sleep	#2 Movement	#3 Nutrition	#4 Connection	#5 Quiet time	#6 Clear thinking
I	I	I	I	I	I
2	2	2	2	2	2
3	3	3	3	3	3
4	4	4	4	4	4
5	5	5	5	5	5
6	6	6	6	6	6
7	7	7	7	7	7
8	8	8	8	8	8
9	9	9	9	9	9
10	10	10	10	10	10

DAY 12: FALL IN LOVE WITH FAILURE

James Prochaska was a teenager when his father died. Prochaska Senior had a deep mistrust of the medical profession and would deny his depression and alcoholism in order to avoid the system. His family were desperate to help him recover. But nothing worked. When his poor dad finally passed, James vowed to find ways to help others make change without the need of psychotherapy. In his book *Changing for Good,* James tells us how he started out on a mission: "I wanted to find some way to bring the wonderful insights of psychology to the mass of people who don't ordinarily benefit from them, those people who are self-changers."

I like people on a mission. They are motivated to do amazing things and James Prochaska did exactly that. He created a scientific model of how people change, called the Transtheoretical Model or Stages of Change Model. His research demonstrated that we move through five stages before we make lasting behavioural change: he called them precontemplation, contemplation, preparation, action and maintenance. The model looks like a perfect circle and the research suggests you cannot skip a stage: you have to move through the process in one perfect circle. My initial assumption was that all the normal people, who were not broken like me, were doing precisely that. But then I read one of Prochaska's research papers and I finally cracked the motivational code.

You see, Prochaska's model revealed a great secret. The circle was not perfect. There was another stage, which he named relapse. On average it would take people four or five times around the Stages of Change loop before they made lasting change. This meant that almost everyone was slipping up, or relapsing, and then moving around the stages again until they eventually made lasting change. It was not a circle, but more of a corkscrew of change. This "changed" everything for me. For the first time in my life I realized that failure, slips, blips and stumbles are part of the process. They do not mean you're a loser; they are baked into change. Failure is not something to run from or be scared of; it's part of your process. I will go a step further: for many of us, it is the most important part of the process.

Own the wins and the losses

This whole 28-day masterclass is designed to get you into a mindset of extreme ownership of your motivation so that you own it all: the wins and the losses, the good and the bad. When you move toward your goals with this mindset you become unstoppable.

And today is when you're going to fall in love with failure. Some brilliant research from Strava, the world's largest social network for athletes, shows that day 12 is the time when most people lose motivation and give up on their exercise goals. After analysing millions of athletes who set a New Year's resolution to get fit, the Strava researchers found a steep decline in activity around 12 January.

This makes sense, because 99 per cent of the planet run their goals on willpower and, as you know, after a couple of weeks willpower runs out.

So how can you push past the day 12 pitfall?

How to own your failure

Here's a simple, three-step approach:

1 Remember a time when you failed in the past. Connect with the feelings, sensations and emotions of this slip-up. Make the picture vivid in your mind. Start to notice the type of negative internal chatter that was present after your mistake. How would you describe those words and emotions?

2 Now, with those emotions swirling around your mind, can you think of other people who have made mistakes or failed, only to rise stronger? Notice how the strength of your emotions and the volume of your inner voice start to fade.

3 Finally, imagine that a member of your dream boat crew (see page 133) made the same mistake. What advice would you give them? How would you encourage them to keep reaching for their goal?

If you rehearse this technique several times you will be prepared for when things go wrong, because they will. You will be ready for failure and now there is nothing that can stop you, because you are taking ownership of your motivation, so it's all learning.

You'll like this

The Strava team don't want you to join the army of day 12 quitters, so they mined the data to provide more valuable motivational insights. Here are the top five things that motivated people to stay active up to ten months later:

⫻ Joining a tribe	46 %
⫻ Setting a goal	92 %
⫻ Finding a buddy	22 %
⫻ Exercising while commuting (running, cycling to work)	43 %
⫻ Getting up early to exercise	43 %

You will notice that all these suggestions appear in the course of this book. The Strava research is based on physical exercise, but can easily be applied to whatever challenge you choose.

DAY 12 CHECK-IN

My goal is ....
.

TIME
A
AT
STEP
ONE
GOAL

GOAL DATE

__/__/__

1. Morning power question
What can I do today to improve my motivational process? ....
....

2. Evening check-in
Did I do my best to [insert goal step] today? What did I do? ....
....

3. Streak checkbox

4. Score your positivity streams

#1 Sleep	#2 Movement	#3 Nutrition	#4 Connection	#5 Quiet time	#6 Clear thinking
1	1	1	1	1	1
2	2	2	2	2	2
3	3	3	3	3	3
4	4	4	4	4	4
5	5	5	5	5	5
6	6	6	6	6	6
7	7	7	7	7	7
8	8	8	8	8	8
9	9	9	9	9	9
10	10	10	10	10	10

DAY 13: FIND A TRIBE

Tribes are key to motivation. Take my friend Joe De Sena, who was a successful broker on Wall Street but felt disconnected. Long hours and late nights with clients had left him unhappy and disillusioned. There was something missing in his life that the fast-paced world of finance didn't offer. He couldn't pinpoint it at the time, but he was missing his tribe.

So Joe quit his job in search of meaning and he found a tribe of ultra athletes who motivated him to test his physical and mental limits. Joe would admit himself that he was not a natural athlete and his transition from desk job to extreme, crazy, insane, nutty-as-a-fruit-cake type of endurance events was tough. But he had a tribe, and it was this togetherness that consistently pushed him to go a little further. The ultra tribe swapped training plans and nutritional ideas, and formed a club for the inspired few. A powerful camaraderie flowed through the community and led to Joe competing in the seemingly impossible Ukatak ultra race.

The Ukatak is held in the middle of the Canadian winter across 350km (220 miles) of desolate frozen landscape. Very few even complete the race, which involves hiking, climbing, biking and running often through knee-deep snow. Joe crossed the finish line having achieved what he once believed impossible.

In this moment he had an epiphany. This was not about endurance; this was about taking life to a whole new level. And he wanted to share this feeling with millions of people. So he set about creating a massive tribe who would motivate one another to achieve the impossible and, in doing so, transform their lives. It's called Spartan and it's now the world's largest obstacle and endurance tribe, with over one million participants taking part in over 30 different countries. When I asked Joe why he believed the Spartan tribe was so important to motivation, his reply said it all: "When you look around at the finish line and see the Spartans, there is a bond than can't be broken. We inspire each other as a team."

As you move through this book you will see tribes everywhere, motivating people like you to achieve their dreams. Today is all about aligning with a group who will hold you accountable and create positive pressure to reach your goals.

What do tribes mean for motivation?

Some great research from Jessica Nolan of the University of Arkansas and her team exposed a group of California residents' seemingly altruistic efforts as just following the crowd. When asked why they liked to save energy, the residents offered those nice rational, human-brain statements like "to protect the environment", "to help future generations" and "to save money".

To test these polite motivations, the research team handed out various motivational door hangers. Some had slogans such as "Protect your environment", while others read "99 per cent of your community turn lights off to save energy". The researchers checked the residents' energy bills before and after the test. When the results came back, they were clear: the only intervention that actually motivated the residents to cut back on energy consumption was not a lovely rational, human reason, but the primitive one of "everyone else is doing it".

Doing what others are doing is a huge motivation. Why? It provides a sense that you must be doing the right thing.

When we align with the right group or tribe, we allow the positive social pressure to motivate us to do the right thing. Let's make peace with the fact that we are all influenced by others. So take control of this powerful motivator and use it with skill. Whenever you have a motivational challenge, align with a tribe that supports your aims and goals. If you are serious about losing weight, find a group to inspire you. If you want to get fit, perhaps join your local park run. If you have a goal of public speaking, Toastmasters is a fantastic tribe that will motivate you toward your goal.

Each new goal is a golden opportunity to be a part of a new crowd, one that's aligned with who you are and who you want to become. And the bonus is that you will build more meaningful connections.

DAY 13 CHECK-IN

My goal is ....
.

```
        ╭──────╮
        │ GOAL │
        ╰──────╯
   TIME ┌────┐
      A ┌┘    │
     AT┌┘     │
  STEP┌┘      │
  ONE┌┘       │       GOAL DATE
 ┌───┘        │
 │            │       __/__/__
```

1. Morning power question
What can I do today to improve my motivational process? ....
....

2. Evening check-in
Did I do my best to [insert goal step] today? What did I do? ....
....

3. Streak checkbox ☐

4. Score your positivity streams

#1 Sleep	#2 Movement	#3 Nutrition	#4 Connection	#5 Quiet time	#6 Clear thinking
1	1	1	1	1	1
2	2	2	2	2	2
3	3	3	3	3	3
4	4	4	4	4	4
5	5	5	5	5	5
6	6	6	6	6	6
7	7	7	7	7	7
8	8	8	8	8	8
9	9	9	9	9	9
10	10	10	10	10	10

DAY 14: ACTIVATE
THE GREATEST MOTIVATOR

During my quest to learn more about motivation, I was intrigued to find out how people found the motivation to overcome serious addiction. You might be thinking, "I just want to learn a language or save for a house", but we can learn a lot from those who have dug deeper and freed themselves from addiction.

When I looked beneath the different techniques to help those with addictions, there was one thing that stood out. The ultimate motivator that had cured so many horrific addictions was love.

Not love in a fluffy "all you need is love" kind of way, but that raw, visceral love of family. My hero in the addiction space, a superb researcher called Stanton Peele, tells us how it is in his book *Recover*: "Prioritizing parental love has cured more addictions than all other 'methods' in the history of addiction combined – and will always do so."

So, wherever possible, link your goals to those you love. Think about ways that you can attach your goal quest to the people who matter most to you. Will your goal to get fit benefit your children who want a parent who is still alive and healthy when they get married? Will your goal to write your book make your parents proud? That sort of thing. Love is the power-positive emotion. You can move mountains on love alone.

And don't forget, as Nicholas Christakis shows us (see page 130), your actions will flow to those you love, and to the people they love and the people *they* love. If you want your partner to drink less, use your motivational superpowers to drink less yourself. If you're concerned about your parents' weight, rather than lecture them, use the motivational process to lose weight yourself. If you're a parent and want to inspire your children to stay fit, slim and healthy, use the motivational mastery to embody these things and do it for the kids. The ultimate motivator is often right under your nose. All you have to do is show up and perform your goal step for that special someone.

DAY 14 CHECK-IN

My goal is ....

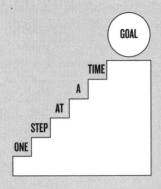

GOAL

TIME
A
AT
STEP
ONE

GOAL DATE

__/__/__

1. Morning power question
What can I do today to improve my motivational process? ....
....

2. Evening check-in
Did I do my best to [insert goal step] today? What did I do? ....
....

3. Streak checkbox

4. Score your positivity streams

#1 Sleep	#2 Movement	#3 Nutrition	#4 Connection	#5 Quiet time	#6 Clear thinking
1	1	1	1	1	1
2	2	2	2	2	2
3	3	3	3	3	3
4	4	4	4	4	4
5	5	5	5	5	5
6	6	6	6	6	6
7	7	7	7	7	7
8	8	8	8	8	8
9	9	9	9	9	9
10	10	10	10	10	10

What you learned this week

Day 8 – Love and kindness: a powerful meditation – and remember to watch out for the delivery guy

Day 9 – The subconscious saboteur: remove your ambivalence, remove willpower

Day 10 – Go green: take a green shower and power up your motivation

Day 11 – Your inner cheerleader: clean up your inner chatter

Day 12 – Failure is part of the process: slip-ups are a sign that you're on the right track

Day 13 – Unlock the power of a tribe: for every goal there is a tribe waiting to motivate you

Day 14 – The greatest motivator: connect your goal to someone you love – it's all you need

See how far you've come

The real power of this week was to help you to find a little kindness for yourself. There are two reasons why this is important. First we are all perfectly imperfect humans. So cut yourself some slack. Life is not perfect, it's bloody tough at times. And you will make mistakes and fumble – this is part of the excitement. If no one ever slipped, life would be so dull.

The second reason is that you *will* fail as soon as you are brave enough to step outside your comfort zone into the growth zone. But that does not mean you should give up. It's a sign that you're on the right track. It will hurt, but in the struggle lies growth, learning and, as you have discovered, happiness. So you can stop beating yourself up, smile more, laugh more, feel more content as you crush your goals. Oh, and by doing so you will inspire those people you love to be a little better. What could be more fulfilling than this?

And the exciting part? You now have two weeks of motivational mastery under your belt and the best bits are still to come.

Week 3 – All About the Marshmallows

This week is critical because the early glow from all those reasons why you want to achieve your goal can start to wear off. This is where the rubber meets the road, and eating marshmallows is the sustenance you need to keep going.

In week 3 you'll discover a major motivational secret: the motivation required to start and the motivation to keep showing up are totally different. And the way you find the motivation to keep going is to stop resisting marshmallows and start eating them.
   Let's do this.

DAY 15: USE "WHYS" TO GET YOU STARTED

One bright Sunday November morning, Ross Edgley emerged from the ocean and staggered onto Margate beach in Kent, southeast England. Edgley had just swum the whole circumference of the United Kingdom – he even slept on the support boat to avoid setting foot on dry land.

He'd covered a distance of 2,910km (1,791 miles). As far as swimming from London to Moscow, or from San Francisco to Dallas. Just imagine the motivation it took to show up 157 days on the trot and swim for 12 hours, through jellyfish stings, deadly whirlpools and storms. Edgley kept on swimming though his body was breaking down – chunks of his tongue had started to fall off due to the salt water. But somehow he achieved the impossible.

How? Edgley revealed that his motivation to start the challenge was different to the motivation he needed to keep going. Initially, he was filled with those typical reasons "why". He wanted to make his family proud, to set a world record, to test the limits of human endurance. But after just a few days of swimming, his motivation had totally changed. Those nice reasons "why" floated away.

Instead of looking to his future "whys", his motivational focus was locked in the present moment. After a few days he was driven forward by the lure of food, sleep, warmth and companionship. So he adapted his plan. His new mission was to "get in and swim" long enough to reach the reward of food, sleep, warmth and time with his crew. Motivation had changed and Ross had adapted. This was the key to achieving the impossible.

Motivation changes

Ross's story helped unlock a major breakthrough for me: the motivation to start is different from the motivation to keep going. For years I made the mistake of assuming they were the same thing.

The fuel to start my goal was lots of reasons why I wanted to achieve it. I clung to those same reasons to keep me going. But after a few days or weeks, my "whys" were no longer enough. My motivation would stall and yet another goal would vanish.

But then I figured it out – if motivation changed, I needed two types of motivation. One to get going and the other to *keep* going.

Why "whys" are great to get you started

The human brain loves those aspirational reasons why you should go after a goal.

There are two types of "whys" and both pull on the emotional levers of pleasure and pain that you discovered in chapter 8.

Pleasure "whys" are all those wonderful positive reasons why you want to achieve your goal:
- I want to run a marathon to make my kids proud
- I want to look great in my wedding dress in six months
- I want to get fit to stay healthy
- I want to write this book to show myself that I can do it

Pain "whys" are the consequences if you don't achieve this goal:
- If I don't lose weight, I will get type 2 diabetes
- If I don't stop drinking, I will lose my family
- If I don't write the blog, I will be stuck in a job I hate

For years traditional motivational gurus have leveraged the concept of pleasure and pain "whys" to motivate millions to get started. Hurray. But when the going gets tough, they stop. Booo. This is because the gurus missed the most important part. Once you get started you need a new motivation to keep going.

But what about finding a big enough "why"?

I totally agree that if you find a big enough reason why, you barely need motivation. But just like finding endless willpower, this happens very infrequently to very few.

Finding a big enough "why" is like backing a horse at odds of 10000/1. It might come in, but it's a massive long shot. This is why the great "why" long shot and the willpower myth leave so many people feeling like failures. Hard as they try, they can't find that one superpowered "why" and they run out of willpower. So they assume they are broken and give up.

I do not want you to do this.

That's why this masterclass is designed for those who don't have a super-duper "why" and are hopeless at willpower, which is basically everyone.

Before I show you how to unlock a new kind of motivation, let's give those pleasure and pain "whys" one last blast. I want you to list all those reasons why you want to achieve this goal. You can make two lists – pleasure "whys" and pain "whys".

Pleasure   **Pain**

. . . .

. . . .

. . . .

. . . .

. . . .

Take a few minutes to suck up the motivational boost this exercise provides, because tomorrow it's time to change the motivational game and eat the marshmallows.

DAY 15 CHECK-IN

My goal is ....
.

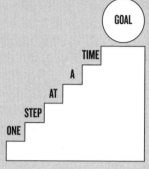

GOAL DATE

__ / __ / __

1. Morning power question

What can I do today to improve my motivational process? ....

....

2. Evening check-in

Did I do my best to [insert goal step] today? What did I do? ....

....

3. Streak checkbox

4. Score your positivity streams

#1 Sleep	#2 Movement	#3 Nutrition	#4 Connection	#5 Quiet time	#6 Clear thinking
1	1	1	1	1	1
2	2	2	2	2	2
3	3	3	3	3	3
4	4	4	4	4	4
5	5	5	5	5	5
6	6	6	6	6	6
7	7	7	7	7	7
8	8	8	8	8	8
9	9	9	9	9	9
10	10	10	10	10	10

DAY 16: MEET THE MARSHMALLOW MAKER

As we saw yesterday, the reason 99.9 per cent of people give up on their goals is that motivation changes and they don't change with it. Your lovely reasons "why" get you started but fade once the novelty wears off. At this point, without a plan, you will start to see the metaphorical I-can't-be-arsed-to-run marshmallow or the I'm-too-tired-to-write marshmallow or the I'll-do-it-tomorrow marshmallow. And your primitive brain will want to eat it. Your only option, like the children in the original marshmallow study, is to use willpower to delay the gratification of *not* running or writing or doing it tomorrow. But as we know, most of us are terrible at delaying gratification and willpower runs out.

Now imagine, rather than letting your primitive brain decide what marshmallows it sees, you create your own healthy marshmallows that you don't have to resist. Your human and primitive brains become aligned because they both want the same thing. Zero willpower is required.

Remember...

...if you don't have a plan for healthy marshmallows, the wrong ones show up.

The most important thing to know about healthy marshmallows is that they are always focused on the present moment. Your primitive brain doesn't care about saving marshmallows for the future. It wants marshmallows now. So make sure the new healthy metaphorical marshmallows you create are based on the experience in the moment.

As you read the examples on the following page, feel the difference in motivation. You can almost sense the power of this idea coming to life as the marshmallow focus is flipped from the unhealthy to the healthy.

CASE STUDY:

ROB'S GOAL: TO GET FIT (EXAMPLE 1)

Rob had a long list of conventional reasons that motivated him to start moving his body: I might get ill if I don't, I want to shape up, I want to be a better role model for my kids.

Trouble is, all those great reasons why Rob should go to the gym weren't enough to motivate him to put on his trainers when he could be watching *Line of Duty*. After a few days, the buzz of motivation from those sensible reasons had gone. So Rob had to find a new motivation to move his body.

At this point, conventional motivation prompts you to reconnect with and cling to your "whys". But it was too late. All Rob could see was a gigantic I-can't-be-arsed-to-exercise marshmallow. And his primitive brain wanted to eat it. So his only option was willpower, which led to him giving up on his goal.

Let's look at the same goal again. But this time, Rob takes control of the marshmallows.

ROB'S GOAL: TO GET FIT (EXAMPLE 2)

To start with, Rob was encouraged to stack the marshmallows in his favour wherever possible by selecting a goal task that he enjoyed.

If you're aiming to get fit, it will be much easier to find healthy marshmallows if you already enjoy the form of physical exercise you're doing. So if you don't like running, don't run. Likewise, if you enjoy walking, then walk. Or if you love swimming, then swim. Rob chose walking because he could listen to podcasts and build this movement into his morning commute.

Rob was instructed to keep any new marshmallows present-moment focused, because the primitive brain always wants instant gratification. So Rob was encouraged to highlight any benefits he experienced while actually performing the goal task. Like this:

- Marshmallow 1: when I move I find I have more energy
- Marshmallow 2: I've got a sense of getting fitter as I walk
- Marshmallow 3: I love being in the fresh air
- Marshmallow 4: I can learn and expand my mind as I move

Suddenly, Rob's movement goal felt totally different. Switching the marshmallows had changed the motivational game completely. He no longer had to find cast-iron willpower to resist the I-can't-be-arsed-to-run marshmallow. He simply changed focus by flipping the marshmallows and trained his brain to want his new healthy marshmallows.

Here's the bonus – when the much stronger primitive brain decides it wants the right thing, it will motivate the rational side of your brain even more. It's a virtuous marshmallow circle.

Life is an experiment. It might take a few goes to connect with your new healthy marshmallows, but keep going until both your brains accept them fully.

Today, list all the positives you experience while performing your goal step. Please dig deep – you will always find some positive marshmallows in the moment if you look hard enough. Try to come up with about five. And if there genuinely aren't any, don't worry. On day 18 I'll show you how to create marshmallows where none exist.

From now on, add your marshmallows to your morning journal. You can put your healthy marshmallows inside the goal steps or whatever suits you. But be sure to connect with these marshmallows on a daily basis, every day until you reach your goal. And remember: change your marshmallows, change your life.

DAY 16 CHECK-IN

My goal is ....
.

GOAL

TIME

A

AT

STEP

ONE

My daily marshmallows

1. ....

2. ....

3. ....

GOAL DATE

__/__/__

1. Morning power question

What can I do today to improve my motivational process? ....

....

2. Evening check-in

Did I do my best to [insert goal step] today? What did I do? ....

....

3. Streak checkbox

4. Score your positivity streams

#1 Sleep	#2 Movement	#3 Nutrition	#4 Connection	#5 Quiet time	#6 Clear thinking
1	1	1	1	1	1
2	2	2	2	2	2
3	3	3	3	3	3
4	4	4	4	4	4
5	5	5	5	5	5
6	6	6	6	6	6
7	7	7	7	7	7
8	8	8	8	8	8
9	9	9	9	9	9
10	10	10	10	10	10

DAY 17: RECOGNIZE AND AVOID MARSHMALLOWS IN DISGUISE

Every part of this programme is designed to give you control of your motivational destiny. As you know, if you don't have a plan then someone, something or evolution has a plan for you. It's the exact same with your marshmallows. If you leave it to chance, your primitive brain gets to choose what it sees. And very often the marshmallows it sees are the wrong ones. They look tasty but they destroy motivation.

The I-can't-be-arsed marshmallow is the most common marshmallow in disguise. Evolution wants to conserve energy. So a goal task that feels as though it will zap too much life-saving energy will produce the I-can't-be-arsed marshmallow.

This is where the whole motivational plan comes together. The higher your six stream scores, the more energy you'll have. If you're sleeping well, eating a nutritious diet, moving your body and not drinking too much, you'll be infused with extra energy, so the I-can't-be-arsed marshmallow appears less often. When you combine this bonus energy with the new healthy marshmallows you made yesterday, the I-can't-be-arsed marshmallow vanishes. So you find the energy and connect with your new type of motivation to write the blog, run, study or find connection and consistently perform your goal step.

However, marshmallows in disguise can still show up when you are in the wrong physical and mental state. The I-can't-be-arsed marshmallow can suddenly reappear when you're thinking about a goal step that requires a different state from the one you're currently in.

A classic example is when you remember you should be exercising, which requires an upbeat, energized disposition, but this thought comes to you when you are in a chilled state relaxing in front of the TV. Or when you're mentally drained after a long day at work and you think about your goal step of studying, which requires an energized, switched-on state.

In these moments the I-can't-be-arsed marshmallow can make a comeback. Unless you have a plan. And this is where state change comes in.

State change is your ability to move from one mental state to another. Have you ever found yourself saying, "I got myself in a right state" when you overreacted or lost your temper? Our emotional state or mood is how we feel in the moment. Sometimes we are in a happy, vibrant state; sometimes we are chilled and relaxed; other times we are angry or fed up. And there are a thousand shades in between. State is vitally important to motivation because certain activities require a certain state. The skill is to learn how to change your state to match your goal task. When you align the right state with the right goal task, the chances of your finding the motivation to take action are exponentially higher.

The guru of state change, Tony Robbins, whom we met on day 10, suggests that one of the best ways to influence your state is to move your body. Motion can create positive emotions which help you find a new perspective. Very often, once your physical state is changing, you can reconnect with your goal step and then execute it.

Once your body is moving and your brain is engaging, take 30 seconds to think about all your positive marshmallows. This combination of physical movement and mental connection will help propel you into action and your goal momentum will be maintained.

Move your body, change your state and follow the plan

Try the exercise below to change state:

- Start from sitting or standing, with your shoulders bent inward toward your chest, and your back bowed.
- Let your arms and hands swing down by your sides. Lower your head in line with your shoulders. Basically you are going for the sulky teenager posture.
- Quickly, make a mental note of how you feel in this position. I would wager you don't feel dynamic.
- Uncurl from this position. Bring your shoulders back.
- Raise your head. Imagine a nice straight line from the top of your head to the bottom of your spine.
- Pull your shoulders back, let your arms relax, keep your head up and look forward.
- If you are sitting down, stand up.

- Take a big full breath as you stand tall. This posture is bright and alert.

How do you feel about your goal step now?

The tomorrow-I'll-be-perfect marshmallow

If you don't have a plan for today, your primitive brain will see the tomorrow-I'll-be-perfect marshmallow. When willpower runs out, you skip the spin class, eat the cake and forget the study because tomorrow-I'll-be-perfect.

In her book *Maximum Willpower*, health psychologist Kelly McGonigal tells the story of a mystery at McDonald's. When the fast-food giant first introduced more healthy options to their menu, there were reports of something strange happening. Rather than salads pushing out the burgers, sales of Big Macs went through the roof.

Having heard about the Big Mac mystery, researchers from Baruch College, New York, created a series of tests to find out why on earth displaying healthy options would lead people to take the unhealthier one. The researchers created various menus containing the usual fast-food options from burgers to nuggets. However, half of the menus also included a salad. The participants were told to select just one option.

The researchers found that whenever a salad was an option, a higher percentage of diners would choose the most unhealthy item on the menu. This study revealed a fundamental flaw in our thinking. We believe, wrongly, that tomorrow we'll be perfect. So today we can be naughty. Just seeing the salad option would produce a sense of goal achievement: the participants believed that they had the power of total rational control to eat the burger today, because tomorrow they would eat the salad. But when tomorrow comes it feels just like today and another goal step is missed because tomorrow we'll be perfect.

This is why you need a plan. If you have mapped out today's goal step, then execute it – today. Do not have a conversation with yourself, because you will lose. There are no rollovers or tomorrow-I'll-be-perfects, because this is a marshmallow in disguise. If you hear your primitive brain shouting, "Do it tomorrow", remember this session, ignore its cries and do it today.

DAY 17 CHECK-IN

My goal is...
.

My daily marshmallows

1...

2...

3...

GOAL DATE

_ _ / _ _ / _ _

1. Morning power question
What can I do today to improve my motivational process?...
....

2. Evening check-in
Did I do my best to [insert goal step] today? What did I do?...
....

3. Streak checkbox

4. Score your positivity streams

#1 Sleep	#2 Movement	#3 Nutrition	#4 Connection	#5 Quiet time	#6 Clear thinking
1	1	1	1	1	1
2	2	2	2	2	2
3	3	3	3	3	3
4	4	4	4	4	4
5	5	5	5	5	5
6	6	6	6	6	6
7	7	7	7	7	7
8	8	8	8	8	8
9	9	9	9	9	9
10	10	10	10	10	10

DAY 18: MAKE YOUR MARSHMALLOW JAR

Since retiring from the Navy SEALs, the elite special ops unit of the US Navy, David Goggins has run ultra marathons for fun and holds the world record for the most pull-ups in 24 hours (4,030, if you fancy taking on the challenge).

When you read a bio like that, it is easy to assume the man was destined to be a warrior. And this is why I love his story, because the young Goggins was a motivational disaster.

A brutal childhood left him on the verge of becoming another crime statistic. His abusive dad would make David and his brother work through the night in the family business and send them to school with virtually no sleep. Finally, his mum had the courage to break free, but this meant she and the kids were fighting to stay afloat. When David's story does finally start to change, you assume he will make a Hollywood rise from zero to hero.

But he doesn't. After failing the entrance examination for the US Air Force several times, he keeps coming back and eventually scrapes in. After four years he leaves the military and ends up depressed and weighing almost 140kg (300lb). Somehow he finds the courage to try for the elite Navy SEALs. At first he is ignored and then laughed at. But one recruiter believes in him and sometimes that's all we need.

That's why this book is one gigantic message – that you can do it. You can achieve any goal you set, when you have a plan and show up.

Which is exactly what Goggins did. Because there was a catch. He would have to lose over 45kg (100lb) in three months to be considered for Navy SEAL selection. It was this goal that kick-started a motivational plan that transformed his life.

A few months later and 45kg (100lb) lighter, Goggins had achieved the impossible. He was accepted to the Navy Seal selection process or Basic Underwater Demolition/SEAL (BUD/S), which is 24 weeks of hell designed to sift out the true warriors.

And he failed again. Not once, but twice. It was only on his third attempt that he made it through and by this time he was a motivational machine.

THIS IS MY POINT: YOU CAN FIND POSITIVE MARSHMALLOWS ANYWHERE IF YOU LOOK HARD ENOUGH

Goggins had discovered the power of a plan. He knew failure was part of the process and that motivation was a skill that anyone could learn. He even managed to make marshmallows out of his pain. When he reached that place where most people give up, he was able to turn the pain into a positive marshmallow, because he was on a mission to be the toughest man on the planet. This is my point: you can find positive marshmallows anywhere if you look hard enough.

Goggins did not make a meteoric rise from nowhere. He stumbled, fumbled, slipped and tripped. But he kept coming back and showing up every day. And slowly, step after step, he transformed his mind, body and life. This is the power of a motivational plan.

Goggins then decided to run an ultra marathon to raise money for the families of fallen servicemen and women. The Badwater-135 ultra marathon is one of the toughest races in the world. But once more Goggins faced a major hurdle: he was told he couldn't enter it unless he had already competed in a race over 162km (100 miles). So a few days later, without even having completed a standard 42km (26-mile) marathon, Goggins ran 163km (101 miles) in 17 hours and qualified for Badwater. In 2006, aged 31, he came fifth out of 85 in the Badwater-135, which was deemed impossible for a novice.

There's more. After falling ill, Goggins had a medical that revealed a major hole in his heart, which meant he had accomplished the impossible on numerous occasions with half the engine that most people have. Having made a full recovery, he continues to do the impossible and inspires millions to do the same. If Goggins can do it – so can you. All you need is a marshmallow jar.

The marshmallow jar

During David's difficult childhood, his loving mother always made sure there were cookies in the jar, no matter what the family chaos. So later in life he created a mental cookie jar of his own past victories. He filled it with those triumphs when he had overcome failure and hardships in order to succeed. Then, when he found himself in so much pain that even his positive marshmallows had vanished, he would reach into his metaphorical cookie jar for help.

In one of the most motivational books you will ever read, *Can't Hurt Me*, Goggins tells us what's in his cookie jar:

When I had to study three times as hard as anybody else during my senior year in high school just to graduate. That was a cookie. Or when I passed the ASVAB test as a senior and then again to get into BUD/S. Two more cookies. I remembered dropping over a hundred pounds in under three months, conquering my fear of water, graduating BUD/S at the top of my class, and being named Enlisted Honor Man in Army Ranger School… All those were cookies loaded with chocolate chunks.

Whenever he was really struggling during a goal, he would reach into the cookie jar in his mind and take out a past victory to motivate him in the present.

This is a superpower motivational idea. Because we forget. We forget what we've already achieved against the odds. We forget how we have already overcome so many trials to reach our place in life. Today, sticking with our theme of marshmallows rather than cookies, I want you to remember and fill up your own jar of past victories that you can pull out when you're in need of motivation.

So, take out your journal and write down all those obstacles you have overcome. Feel free to go back to childhood if that works for you, because it all counts. List as many as you can to fill up your jar. Then step back, look at all you have achieved and know that you can do it – because you already have.

DAY 18 CHECK-IN

My goal is...

GOAL

STEP AT A TIME ONE

My daily marshmallows

1..

2..

3..

GOAL DATE

__/__/__

1. Morning power question

What can I do today to improve my motivational process?..

....

2. Evening check-in

Did I do my best to [insert goal step] today? What did I do?...

....

3. Streak checkbox

4. Score your positivity streams

#1 Sleep	#2 Movement	#3 Nutrition	#4 Connection	#5 Quiet time	#6 Clear thinking
1	1	1	1	1	1
2	2	2	2	2	2
3	3	3	3	3	3
4	4	4	4	4	4
5	5	5	5	5	5
6	6	6	6	6	6
7	7	7	7	7	7
8	8	8	8	8	8
9	9	9	9	9	9
10	10	10	10	10	10

DAY 19: GIVE MARSHMALLOWS AWAY TO GET THEM BACK

When I first met Catherine Gray, author of the brilliant *The Unexpected Joy Of Being Sober*, we instantly bonded. Our experience of going alcohol-free had motivated us to share our stories to inspire others. In doing so we unleashed thousands of positive marshmallows as people started to share with us how our stories had inspired them. In giving our marshmallows away, we received many more in return or, as Catherine put it, "being open, honest and sharing my story [had] such a positive impact on other people, which continually inspires me at the same time."

I cannot stress too often how powerful this is. And it's not about inspiring millions – you start with one. This could be a friend, a member of a group, a colleague or someone random. The key is to share a bit of your story. The beautiful paradox of giving is that when we help others we help ourselves. Motivation is no different. When we motivate others, we motivate ourselves.

Today I want you to give your positive marshmallows away to help others, and collect even more marshmallows in return. For example, if your motivational goal is to walk 5km (3 miles), could you volunteer at your local park run to help motivate others to do the same? Or if your goal is to become a personal development coach, could you find an online forum or someone you know and offer them support and guidance?

Barbara Fredrickson is Professor of Psychology at North Carolina University, and my positivity hero. Her research and her books, especially *Positivity: Groundbreaking Research to Release Your Inner Optimist and Thrive*, have transformed the way we view kindness, positivity and motivation. If Martin Seligman, whom we will meet on page 235, is the grandfather of positive psychology, Fredrickson is the grandma.

Fredrickson developed the "broaden and build" theory of positive emotions, which suggests that "unlike negative emotions, which narrow people's ideas about possible actions, positive emotions do the opposite: They broaden people's ideas about possible actions, opening our awareness to a wider range of thoughts and actions than is typical."

What Fredrickson is telling us is that positive emotions broaden our thinking so that we can see more options. For our ancestors, these emotions sparked the motivation to develop abilities, skills, useful traits and resources that could protect them against future threats. The early humans who embraced these good feelings were better equipped to face adversity, so their genetics kept moving.

And nothing has changed. What worked 70,000 years ago still works today. Positive emotions fuel our motivation to change because we have an inbuilt desire to improve our skills. We want to be prepared to face the future by developing both physical and mental skills. We are also attracted to activities that will facilitate physical fitness and health because, once more, these traits will help us survive any future demands. This makes perfect sense. When we are angry, our focus is all about the moment. We can't see the haystack for the needle. But when we feel joy, gratitude, hope, pride or any positive emotion, we are motivated to unlock new ideas, options and ways of thinking that can transform our lives. The bonus is that these feel-good emotions feel good.

Fredrickson's research offers two major insights into why giving away your marshmallows or performing acts of kindness are great motivators.

When you're aware of your giving, you get more in return
When you're conscious of your kindness, you receive even more positivity back. Keeping a tally of each act of kindness made the positivity of participants in the study considerably great. When we are filled with positive emotions we are able to think outside the box; we're more open to challenges and feel motivated.

Several large acts of giving on one day feed back more positivity
Performing several acts of kindness on a particular day is more powerful than making it commonplace. In another study by Fredrickson and others, participants who displayed normal levels of kindness on typical days, but then selected a particular day to ramp up the kindness, by volunteering for example, experienced more overall positivity.

So, when possible, plan to give your marshmallows away by performing acts of kindness on a specific day of "giving".

Giving for living

The positive bonuses don't end there – some amazing research from the University of Michigan even suggests that when we give to others we live longer.

When you give your marshmallows away, you receive more motivation back in two forms. First, there is the positive glow from helping someone else. Second, you create another level of accountability. Once you're out there helping others, you won't want to let them down. So you receive the bonus of a positive social pressure that will motivate you to keep showing up in order to achieve your goal and inspire others.

You already have a wealth of experience to give and hopefully a platform from which to give it. Whatever your goal, there is a tribe or an individual out there you can help. This is an incredibly important point. When you give you receive, which creates an upward spiral of positivity and motivation.

Your mini challenge for today

Look for opportunities to gift your current positive marshmallows to someone else. If you found a tribe on day 13, think how you could share your motivational experience with one of the group.

If the tribe is online, perhaps create a post or, if you want to ramp up positivity, record a video and share it. Drop someone an email or message. Could you write a blog, or post on LinkedIn? Or phone a friend and let them know how you're getting on? This is not about being preachy, it's just a chance to show a little kindness.

DAY 19 CHECK-IN

My goal is..
.

GOAL

TIME

A

AT

STEP

ONE

My daily marshmallows

1...

2...

3...

GOAL DATE

__ / __ / __

1. Morning power question
What can I do today to improve my motivational process?..
....

2. Evening check-in
Did I do my best to [insert goal step] today? What did I do?...
....

3. Streak checkbox

4. Score your positivity streams

#1 Sleep	#2 Movement	#3 Nutrition	#4 Connection	#5 Quiet time	#6 Clear thinking
1	1	1	1	1	1
2	2	2	2	2	2
3	3	3	3	3	3
4	4	4	4	4	4
5	5	5	5	5	5
6	6	6	6	6	6
7	7	7	7	7	7
8	8	8	8	8	8
9	9	9	9	9	9
10	10	10	10	10	10

DAY 20: UNLOCK MASTERY MARSHMALLOWS

Mastery marshmallows are small wins or signs that you're making progress. From an evolutionary point of view, acquiring a new skill might prove beneficial to survival or reproduction, so your primitive brain likes it. A lot. For this reason, any tangible signs of improvement are extremely motivating. Ryan and Deci, the researchers who created self-determination theory and whom we met on page 90, believe there are three psychological nutriments that are critical to a fully engaged and motivated life.

The first is "autonomy" (which we discussed on page 90) and the second is "relatedness" or connection with others (see page 70). The final nutriment is "competence" or mastery, which is the ability to control the outcome of an activity while mastering a task. Today's session is dedicated to helping you create the right mindset to unleash a bag of mastery marshmallows.

The growth mindset

Carol Dweck is the queen of mindset and Professor of Psychology at Stanford University. Her research has demonstrated that the mindset you adopt can influence your motivation. Dweck identified two types of mindset: a fixed one and a growth one, both of which have a big impact on motivation. Someone with a fixed mindset believes they're either clever or dumb, talented or talentless. They feel measured by failure. They look for signs of progress based on whether they are winning or losing. There is no room for learning from error, because they believe in fixed traits, so they cannot grow.

On the other hand, people with a growth mindset embrace failure as a way to learn. They're not scared of being wrong or asking those "dumb" questions because they understand it's all learning. They don't need to cover up weaknesses or mistakes. They want to continually grow, by challenging themselves to experience new things without fear of being defined by setbacks. They recognize that there is no such thing as failure, only feedback.

According to Dweck's research, people with a growth mindset

strive for bigger goals, experience lower stress, anxiety and depression, have higher performance levels and are more motivated. Ultimately, those with a growth mindset understand that through hard work, determination and practice almost any skill can be mastered.

The growth mindset leads to mastery marshmallows because there is always the opportunity to progress even when things are not going to plan. Your motivational mission is not about being perfect, it's about taking charge of your motivation and learning.

The exciting part, and another stream running through this book, is that everything in your life can be adapted and improved – even your mindset. Dweck has demonstrated that you can build a growth mindset. So you can change both mindset and marshmallows. And in doing so you change your motivation.

It's all material

The growth mindset is not just a mindset for goals, it's a mindset for life. Because everything is learning. Robert Greene, author of *Mastery*, has a saying: "It's all material." As an author, speaker and businessman, Greene believes that every event – good, bad and ugly – has the potential to be used to improve his work.

From this vantage point, he is able to sidestep some of the pain and self-pity when things don't work out, because he is simply collecting data. He sees every obstacle as a gateway to wisdom.

Imagine viewing your daily goal steps and obstacles as opportunities to grow. What if you felt grateful for the annoying colleague, flippant comment or stressful moment because they gift you new insight? This subtle reframe might create the space you need to start loving life, warts and all, because "it's all material". When you combine Greene's approach and a growth mindset, you set up the platform to see momentum marshmallows everywhere. Even when things don't go to plan, you can still find signs that you are growing stronger or making progress because of how you dealt with the stressful situation.

There are two types of mastery marshmallows:

I **Momentum-mastery marshmallows**
Think of momentum-mastery marshmallows as small wins. Today and every day look for the signposts of progress. This

could be a subtle comment from a friend who mentions that you look great, or submitting an essay for the course you're studying. Wherever possible, build markers of success or momentum-mastery marshmallows into your plan. Could you track your progress in some tangible way? Your streak counter (see day 1) is a great example of a momentum-mastery marshmallow. As the days build up, you will experience the buzz of mastery.

Growth-mastery marshmallows

When things go wrong, can you use a growth mindset to find embers of progress? Growth-mastery marshmallows are signs that you're learning and growing through adversity. You are no longer scared of failure because you know it's a sign that you are making progress. Once you connect with this mindset, you will find opportunity to see growth-mastery marshmallows in everything you do.

Today's task

Every time you see a mastery marshmallow, pause and acknowledge your progress. Perhaps physically write the sign of progress down in your journal. Start to notice that your actions are making a positive difference.

The key today is to become aware of any signs of improvement and learning. And remember, the slow march toward mastery is like motivational gold to both your primitive and your human brain.

DAY 20 CHECK-IN

My goal is..

My daily marshmallows

1..

2..

3..

GOAL DATE

__/__/__

I. Morning power question

What can I do today to improve my motivational process?...

....

2. Evening check-in

Did I do my best to [insert goal step] today? What did I do?...

....

3. Streak checkbox

4. Score your positivity streams

#I Sleep	#2 Movement	#3 Nutrition	#4 Connection	#5 Quiet time	#6 Clear thinking
I	I	I	I	I	I
2	2	2	2	2	2
3	3	3	3	3	3
4	4	4	4	4	4
5	5	5	5	5	5
6	6	6	6	6	6
7	7	7	7	7	7
8	8	8	8	8	8
9	9	9	9	9	9
I0	I0	I0	I0	I0	I0

TRYING TO EXERT CONTROL
OVER THE UNCONTROLLABLE
LEADS TO FRUSTRATION,
STRESS AND ANXIETY

DAY 21: CHANGE YOUR THOUGHTS, CHANGE YOUR BEHAVIOUR

About 2,000 years ago, philosopher Epictetus asked his students to list the things that were under their control and those that were not. He looked at their suggestions, and dismissed them all. In his opinion there was only one thing truly under our control: our beliefs. Everything else, to a greater or lesser extent, is out of our hands.

Epictetus was right. We don't have control over loved ones, partners, work or fortune. We don't even have total control over our health. Lots of people who live healthily still get sick. All of these things come and go, like the changing of the tides. Loved ones can pass, partners leave, work dry up and fortune be fickle. That in a nutshell is life, and trying to exert control over the uncontrollable leads to frustration, stress and anxiety.

It was another quote from Epictetus, "Men are disturbed not by things, but by their opinions about them", that inspired psychologist Albert Ellis and psychiatrist Aaron Beck to develop cognitive behavioural therapy (CBT). Of all the talk therapies, CBT now has the most clinical support to suggest that it is as effective as many of the drugs that treat depression and anxiety disorders. However, unlike many drugs, there are few to no side effects.

Based on cognitive behavioural principles, Ellis created the ABC model. First (A) we experience an event, next (B) we interpret that event and finally (C) based on this interpretation we feel an emotional response. Using Epictetus's idea, Ellis concluded that we do have control to alter our usual conditioned response or pattern of behaviour (C) by changing (B) our thoughts or opinions about the event. These simple concepts – CBT and the ABC model – have since transformed the lives of millions of people.

It was a quote from Albert Einstein that finally helped me solve the motivational puzzle: "The most important decision we make is whether we believe we live in a friendly or hostile universe." Epictetus, Einstein and Ellis were all saying the same thing: we have control over what we believe, and this gives us the power to change what we believe to be marshmallows and, in doing so, change our lives.

CASE STUDY:

JERRY DID IT!

Jerry was running his own PR business, but life had plateaued. He had lots of ideas unrelated to his day job, but was struggling to bring them to life. So he decided to take my masterclass to gain a deeper understanding of how he might fire up his personal life and career. What he did not realize was that, a year later, his motivational plan would lead him toward deep meaning and purpose in the most unexpected place.

The masterclass changed so many small things in my life that eventually guided me toward a massive change. First I loved the NEAT concept and how small changes add up to make a big impact. One example is, rather than take a 2-litre (3½-pint) bottle of water into work, I deliberately make myself climb the stairs to get a refill in a smaller cup. On a hot day this might mean six trips up and down the stairs. This might not sound like a lot, but over a year these trips have made a difference. I also used my motivational plan to take a break from alcohol, which turned into a decision to give it up altogether. I've improved my sleep and I get up at 5.30am to work on all my personal projects before the working day begins. These early starts have been a game changer for me, as I work best in the mornings. I lost 3kg (6½lb) in weight and gained a load of extra energy.

The most powerful part of the masterclass was when I created my authentic-self manifesto. This revealed my true values of generosity, fun and hard work. I sort of knew these things, but I had never really expressed them before. I even put this authentic-self statement up on a white board in the office and it's still guiding me today. I know for a fact that I am always most motivated when I am aligned with this statement. These changes and new-found sense of motivation propelled me forward.

When my seven-year-old daughter Charlotte asked, "Why are people so different?" and I fumbled for a decent answer, I had an idea. And I also had a motivational plan to make it happen. I thought there must be millions of kids all wondering the same thing and struggling to find an answer. So I thought, why not create a little fun poem or rap to help explain? I then took this concept and kept building on it. Eventually I found a great illustrator and turned the rap into a book called Spot the Different.

I don't know if this was a subconscious thing, but creating the book was totally inline with my authentic-self statement. It was extremely hard work. I am giving back, as £1 from each sale goes to the Children's Literacy Charity, and best of all I am having a laugh and a lot of fun doing it. I guess this is why I was so motivated to make it happen – because it instinctively feels right and as if I am meant to be doing this.

I could never have predicted that writing a children's book would fill me with such passion and meaning, but here I am. And it all started when I began to understand my motivation and values and created a plan that I would re-use over and over. It's a year since I took the masterclass and now I am an author and have two more books in the pipeline.

DAY 21 CHECK-IN

My goal is..
.

GOAL

STEP ONE AT A TIME

My daily marshmallows

1...

2...

3...

GOAL DATE

__/__/__

1. Morning power question

What can I do today to improve my motivational process?..

....

2. Evening check-in

Did I do my best to [insert goal step] today? What did I do?..

....

3. Streak checkbox

4. Score your positivity streams

#1 Sleep	#2 Movement	#3 Nutrition	#4 Connection	#5 Quiet time	#6 Clear thinking
1	1	1	1	1	1
2	2	2	2	2	2
3	3	3	3	3	3
4	4	4	4	4	4
5	5	5	5	5	5
6	6	6	6	6	6
7	7	7	7	7	7
8	8	8	8	8	8
9	9	9	9	9	9
10	10	10	10	10	10

What you learned this week

Day 15 – Motivation changes: first line up your "whys", then get ready to eat the marshmallows

Day 16 – The marshmallow maker: create and eat your healthy marshmallows

Day 17 – Marshmallows in disguise: avoid the unhealthy ones

Day 18 – The marshmallow jar: dip into past wins to fire up motivation in the present

Day 19 – Give your marshmallows away: help motivate others, to help motivate yourself

Day 20 – Mastery is key: everything is learning. Your mastery mindset unlocks motivation

Day 21 – The most important concept in this book: change your marshmallows, change your life

See how far you've come

Just imagine you now hold the secret to lasting motivation. You
know the secret to making the choices you truly want to make. You
have discovered exactly how to refocus your attention away from
those great reasons why and onto the present-moment positive
marshmallows. I bet you can already feel the difference this subtle
reframe makes. You can almost instantly notice a difference when
you laser in on those benefits. Your primitive brain starts to
re-align with your goal and motivation follows because you no
longer have to resist. You can just let your primitive brain eat the
healthy positive marshmallows and wallow in these small wins.

By now you also know what marshmallows to avoid and how to
reconnect with past victories to motivate yourself in the present.
The kindness theme flows through your learning and this week you
learned how to give your marshmallows away to get motivation
back.

Also at this stage you are setting up the potential for one of the
greatest discoveries – that meaning and purpose come from two
elements: momentum and mastery. Both of which you are now
cultivating in your life. As you progress toward your goals, you
build mastery, which can, very often, unlock hidden meaning. Just
think back to Jerry and his children's books (page 198). It is almost
impossible to figure out your life's purpose from a standing start,
but once you are in motion things start to happen that can reveal
a glimpse of future meaning. It might not happen within this first
28 days, but over the coming months perhaps your purpose in life
will appear. How exciting is this?

Finally this week you have learned the two most powerful
insights from all my years of study, the combination of which will
transform the way you learn the skill of motivation. So if you take
away anything from this book, please remember this:

- ⫯ The motivation to start and the motivation to keep going are
  totally different
- ⫯ Change your marshmallows and you can change your life

Week 4 – Now You're Ninja Level

This life thing is all a game. And mastery of your motivation will give you a belief that you can decide from here on in how you play it. You can absolutely achieve everything you have dreamed of and do it all while having a laugh and loving life. Yes, it will hurt a bit, but it's that nice pain that you get when you're working out. And yes, there will be slips, but as you know this is where the great learning is. This final week is all about taking your skills to the next level. You will learn how to outsource your motivation the right way, get your gut onside and use a mantra from Roman times that will put a rocket up your motivation. And if your goal is not right, you will learn how to switch with your confidence intact. Finally, you will learn the importance of celebrating the right way, before reaching your 28-day goal.

Let's do this.

DAY 22: OUTSOURCE YOUR MARSHMALLOWS BUT OWN THE PLAN

I was chilling on holiday in the Fullerton Hotel, Singapore, lost in the views of the harbour, when an old friend I hadn't seen for years waltzed into the bar. I did a proper double take. Troy was half the man I had once known, in amazing shape and he looked great. The last time I'd met him he was 13kg (28lb) heavier, unfit, unhealthy, stressed out and maxed out. Sound familiar?

As a top solicitor, living the expat lifestyle, Troy hadn't seen a gym for 20 years. But here he was all buff. Intrigued, I wanted to know how he'd done it.

"Simple," he said. "I outsourced my motivation."

Troy had lost all faith in his motivation to get fit. Life was always in the way. Fortunately he was in a position to invest in an elite training programme called Ultimate Performance. His trainer created the plan and motivated him to show up. If you show up enough times and eat what your trainer tells you and do the exercises they show you, the results are impressive.

This is a major point – anything is possible if you show up enough times and execute the daily steps. Whether you want to transform your body, career, bank balance or relationships, it's the same process. But rather than creating his own plan, Troy had outsourced his. All he had to do to get results was keep turning up.

It's an interesting angle. I fully believe you can master the skill of motivation so you never need to outsource. Yet Troy helped me acknowledge the power of outsourcing. We have all been motivated by a coach, mentor, class or group.

The trouble is, I would wager that at some point in life you have lost momentum when outsourced motivation has dried up. Perhaps it was a Zumba class that clashed with your kid's club and suddenly you stopped dancing. Perhaps your piano teacher moved away or your business coaching sessions came to an end. We have all been there. And this is my major issue with outsourcing motivation: what happens when we can no longer afford the coach, or the class gets cancelled, or we leave the tribe?

Too often when we outsource motivation, we also give our motivation away. And without this hired motivational help, nothing happens.

But then I cracked the solution.

Outsourcing motivation works wonderfully when you own it

Rather than outsourcing motivation and giving it away, make it part of your plan. When you take ownership of the outsourced motivation, you can still take the learning.

Your aim is to be empowered enough that you can still execute the goal step even if your coach, trainer, teacher, group or tribe doesn't show up. In this way you own the motivation required to make it happen. The outsourced learning is within your plan, so if a class gets cancelled or the sessions end you can tweak your motivational plan to adapt and find another way to perform your goal steps on your own or with someone else. This is a total reframe from the usual scenario where your motivation is tied to someone else.

My belief is that all trainers, coaches, classes and books should empower you to be able to perform your goal step without any outsourced motivation. The outsourced motivation you choose to add into your plan is bonus motivation that you're in control of, not the other way around.

How to outsource motivation the right way

Today, look for ways to outsource your motivation in the right way to fast-track your goals. Would a coach, mentor, group or tribe inject a new level of motivation? Then include it as part of your plan. Factor these sessions into the relevant goal steps. Then show up, execute and learn everything you can.

Take the instruction with a growth mindset (see page 192). What can you learn from the session? Could you perform the routines or exercises without someone standing over you? Pay attention to the tools, books, weights or equipment you're using. Ask how everything works.

Your mission is to take total ownership of the outsourced process so that you can execute it on your own. As long as you feel empowered, outsourcing motivation can be a fantastic way to reach your dreams.

DAY 22 CHECK-IN

My goal is..
.

My daily marshmallows

1...

2...

3...

GOAL DATE

__/__/__

I. Morning power question
What can I do today to improve my motivational process?...
....

2. Evening check-in
Did I do my best to [insert goal step] today? What did I do?...
....

3. Streak checkbox

4. Score your positivity streams

#I Sleep	#2 Movement	#3 Nutrition	#4 Connection	#5 Quiet time	#6 Clear thinking
I	I	I	I	I	I
2	2	2	2	2	2
3	3	3	3	3	3
4	4	4	4	4	4
5	5	5	5	5	5
6	6	6	6	6	6
7	7	7	7	7	7
8	8	8	8	8	8
9	9	9	9	9	9
I0	I0	I0	I0	I0	I0

DAY 23: GET YOUR GUT ON SIDE

I don't want to freak you out, but right now there are trillions of creatures living in your stomach that have the power to influence your health and behaviour. Have you ever wondered why you feel gutted or have a gut feeling about someone or butterflies in your tummy when you're nervous? It's because we have trillions of microbes in our gut that communicate directly with a network of nerves that pathologist Dr Michael Gershon, in his groundbreaking book of the same name, describes as "The Second Brain".

The collection of microbes that live in your gut includes bacteria, bacteriophages, fungi, protozoa and viruses, and collectively they are called microbiome or gut flora. What's amazing is that there are about ten times more microbial cells in your body than there are human cells.

You might be thinking, what on earth have trillions of microbiomes got to do with motivation? Surely there is no way a single-cell organism is motivating you to change career or learn the piano? But research suggests it might.

Dr John Cryan is the Chair of Anatomy and Neuroscience at University College Cork in Ireland, and also a pioneer in the field of psychobiotics. Psychobi-what-ics? Foods and interventions that positively influence our microbiome and subsequently our health and motivation.

When I first met the jolly Dr Cryan, he told me that research into the microbiome is at a very early stage due to recent advances in DNA sequencing.

"But we do know that studies have demonstrated how microbiome can affect depression and anxiety," he explained. "Research also shows how changes in our microbiome or gut flora can directly influence food choice."

Could these microbes in our gut influence motivation toward our goals? "Absolutely," said Dr Cryan.

And the next discovery blew my tiny mind.

Who ordered the pizza?

I will hand you over to Dr Cryan for this one, as it gets a bit icky. "We have demonstrated in our labs that you can transfer 'the blues'

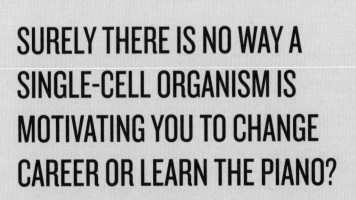

SURELY THERE IS NO WAY A
SINGLE-CELL ORGANISM IS
MOTIVATING YOU TO CHANGE
CAREER OR LEARN THE PIANO?

using gut microbiome," he says. "We transferred fecal matter from humans with depression into rats and the rodents became depressed too."

I'm not suggesting that you queue up outside Tony Robbins's bathroom if you want extra motivation. But what Dr Cryan and his team are demonstrating is the mind-blowing influence microbes have on our behaviour.

In further studies, researchers were able to influence a fruit fly's food choice by changing its microbiome. Scientist Scott Anderson sums up the power of our microbes perfectly in a book he co-authored with Dr Cryan, *The Psychobiotic Revolution*: "Your cravings, it seems, might belong more to the second brain in your gut than the one in your head. Who is really running the show?" Are you really a pizza lover or is your microscopic army ordering a takeaway, and you're just the delivery guy?

Can your microbiome motivate you to save for a house?

The research clearly shows that microbiome can influence anxiety, depression and cravings, so there is a direct link to motivation. When anxious or depressed we are less motivated to achieve our goals.

Although studies are yet to prove a connection between motivation and microbiome in a positive sense – that is, that a healthy gut will help you change career or learn a language – Dr Cryan believes research will soon show that our second brain has a direct influence on the motivation to achieve our personal goals. "Our state of mind is directly influenced by the state of our gut," he says.

My great mate Dr Alan Desmond is a consultant gastroenterologist, One Year No Beer graduate and a self-confessed gut-health nerd. Here are his top five tips to maximize the power of your gut bugs!

Eat a wide variety of plants – our healthy bacteria absolutely love plant fibre. This was confirmed when the American Gut Project analysed the gut microbiomes of over 11,000 volunteers from around the world. This huge scientific effort showed that the key to maintaining a healthy and diverse microbiome is to eat lots of plants and to eat them in variety. Every plant-based food, be it a bean, green or wholegrain, contains different types of fibre and important phytonutrients. Our microbiome loves them all.

Get enough sleep – the bugs of our microbiome seem to work on the same 24-hour daily cycle as the rest of our body. In fact, some researchers believe that our microbiome plays an important role in setting our body clock. Sleep deprivation, jet lag and shift work have all been linked to reduced microbial diversity. Show your microbiome some love by getting seven to eight hours' sleep a night.

Make exercise part of your routine – in 2014 a team of Irish researchers found that elite rugby players displayed an impressive level of microbiome diversity. Further studies have shown that we can all reap the gut-health benefits of regular exercise, which helps to boost levels of healthy fibre-loving bacteria.

Spend time outdoors – a sanitized indoor lifestyle is not the best thing for our microbial health. We know that people who live in the countryside tend to have healthier and more diverse microbiomes than city dwellers. If you can't make it to the great outdoors, spending time in parks or gardens can be of benefit.

Avoid taking unnecessary antibiotics – antibiotics have been of incredible benefit to humankind, helping us fight common serious infections such as pneumonia and meningitis. However, if you have a simple cough or cold which your doctor feels will settle without these drugs, then do your microbiome a favour and take their advice. A single course of antibiotics seriously alters the balance and diversity of the human microbiome. Another way to avoid excess antibiotics is to remove meat and dairy from your diet. The vast majority of antibiotics used in the world are given to farmed animals. These antibiotics remain in the food chain and affect the human microbiome.

The bigger picture

When you zoom out, everything loops back in a motivational circle. Get the basics right, fill up your motivational streams and you set up the perfect motivational platform to achieve your goals. Not only will you have your body and brain on board, you will also engage your second brain, the gut. In doing so you create a vibrant, fully motivated, healthy life. Win-win.

DAY 23 CHECK-IN

My goal is..
.

My daily marshmallows

1...

2...

3...

GOAL DATE

__/__/__

1. Morning power question

What can I do today to improve my motivational process?...

....

2. Evening check-in

Did I do my best to [insert goal step] today? What did I do?...

....

3. Streak checkbox

4. Score your positivity streams

#1 Sleep	#2 Movement	#3 Nutrition	#4 Connection	#5 Quiet time	#6 Clear thinking
1	1	1	1	1	1
2	2	2	2	2	2
3	3	3	3	3	3
4	4	4	4	4	4
5	5	5	5	5	5
6	6	6	6	6	6
7	7	7	7	7	7
8	8	8	8	8	8
9	9	9	9	9	9
10	10	10	10	10	10

DAY 24: MEMENTO MORI

For years I was guilty of rushing out the door every morning with barely a goodbye for my daughters. With my head down I'd charge to the station while dreaming up problems I might face, only to find they never arose.

In my mind, like many of you, I had one of those super-duper important jobs that meant I had to be in work super-duper early to do really important stuff. I was more concerned about getting to the office than spending connected time with my wife and children. My priority was to be seen, to prove that I worked hard. I was running my life on fear and adrenaline.

Holidays were the only time I could switch off and I often got ill, which is a classic sign of stress. You just about hold it together, but when your body finally slows down it reveals the truth – you're exhausted. After a week of rest I would feel better and, armed with a bit of a suntan, would start the same process again.

Slowly but surely I had become totally misaligned with the real priorities in life. The big job had smothered my world. Then I started to learn more about motivation and something wonderful happened.

As my motivational snowball started to roll, I also re-aligned with my real priorities. The wonderful irony was that the less I worried about work and the more I focused on the six streams of positivity, the better my performance in the office.

But I was still rushing out the door, taking my family for granted. Then I read *The Daily Stoic* by modern philosopher Ryan Holiday, and everything changed.

I want to pause here and say that books are one of the greatest sources of motivation you will ever find. Words and ideas have the power to fundamentally change how we view the world. I've lost count of how many times a book has unearthed something that changed me at my core. In my opinion one of the greatest goals you can set is to read more. Hopefully this book is the start.

Right, back to business: discovering what's really important in life. So, a story from *The Daily Stoic* brightened my world. After a great victory, Roman commanders would be celebrated as heroes. It was not uncommon during the victory parade for a great commander to have one of his men whisper into his ear two of the most important words you might ever hear: "Memento mori." In English? "Remember death." Just as the great warrior was flying high on victory and his ego probably running riot, the message was to remember that glory might be gone in a flash.

We tend to forget or ignore the most obvious truth, that at some point we die. This is not about being morbid or sad, it's the very opposite. When we acknowledge that life is fragile, we gift ourselves the motivation to make the most of every day. Why put your life off until tomorrow, if tomorrow might never come? Why rush out the door without saying a real goodbye to the people who matter most?

Memento mori mantra

As part of my journaling ritual I started to write "memento mori" and things began to shift. I no longer rushed out the door in the morning. I took my time to hug my girls as if I meant it, as if it were the last time. I cannot tell you the difference this made. One fully conscious loving embrace was worth a thousand half-hearted efforts. If I did walk out the door and something happened, there would be no regrets, because I would have taken a moment of bliss to love the important things in life.

My new memento mori philosophy started to flow outward. I realized my parents might not be here forever. I could not predict if this might be the last time, so I started to hug them both as if I meant it. They have never said so, but I know they can tell the difference by how they look afterward.

The memento mori mantra is rocket fuel to motivation, because it forces you to embrace every minute of every day as though it might be your last.

Try writing "memento mori" in your journal today and feel its power. Now, ask yourself:

- If today were your last, would you behave differently?
- Would you rush out the door and forget to kiss your loved ones goodbye?
- Would you waste time on a hangover?
- Would you ignore the beauty of nature?
- Would you find forgiveness and peace?

The time machine that we hopped into on page 119 and memento mori work together beautifully. The time machine helps you realize you have more time than you think, while memento mori reminds you that life is fragile, so you should love every moment and not wait for a tomorrow that might never come.

You cannot change the past, but your future is undecided. Now is your time.

DAY 24 CHECK-IN

My goal is ....
.

GOAL

STEP ONE AT A TIME

My daily marshmallows

1. ....

2. ....

3. ....

GOAL DATE

__/__/__

I. Morning power question

What can I do today to improve my motivational process? ....

....

2. Evening check-in

Did I do my best to [insert goal step] today? What did I do? ....

....

3. Streak checkbox

4. Score your positivity streams

#1 Sleep	#2 Movement	#3 Nutrition	#4 Connection	#5 Quiet time	#6 Clear thinking
1	1	1	1	1	1
2	2	2	2	2	2
3	3	3	3	3	3
4	4	4	4	4	4
5	5	5	5	5	5
6	6	6	6	6	6
7	7	7	7	7	7
8	8	8	8	8	8
9	9	9	9	9	9
10	10	10	10	10	10

DAY 25: MAKE FRIENDS WITH FEAR

The number-one thing that will stop you achieving your goal is fear. Fear of what other people think, fear of failure and fear of loss consistently hold us back.

Fear frustrates me because it's a great motivator, but its powers are usually misdirected. Fear-based emotions tend to motivate us to stop performing our goal steps. Embarrassment is fear of what other people think. Saying "I could never do that" is fear of failure. Being scared of change is fear of loss. Your primitive brain sends these fear-laced messages to hold you back because it wants to keep you in your comfort zone where it is safe.

Here's the secret: whenever you imagine fear ahead, it's a sign that you are on the right track. So don't run from fear. Become a hunter of the scary stuff, because your dreams are hidden inside it. "The cave you most fear to enter holds the treasure you seek," wrote the wonderful Joseph Campbell in *The Hero with a Thousand Faces*. Or as Susan Jeffers urges in her book of the same name, "Feel the fear and do it anyway."

I designed this masterclass specifically to help you overcome your fears. At the end of this process there will be no fear-based excuses left. It will still be scary, though. Because, even when you rationally sort through your fears, they do not magically vanish: the fear remains because you're dancing outside your comfort zone. Your aim is to learn to embrace fear and view it as a sign that you are testing yourself by stepping into the growth zone.

Wherever you feel fear, move toward it. It will be frightening. It will test you. But on the other side you might find your dreams.

Overcome your fear of loss

The default fear that we experience as we progress toward a goal is the fear of loss. The primitive brain loves the status quo. It does not like change. So it focuses on losses to try to scare you into stopping. For example:

- If I save money instead of going out, my friends will think I'm boring

SAYING "I COULD NEVER DO THAT" IS FEAR OF FAILURE

- I am missing my Friday night takeaway
- I could be watching TV

The quickest way to shatter loss-based fears is to focus on the wins. If you feel the tug of your primitive brain trying to frighten you into stopping your goal step, pause, acknowledge the fear and then manage it. This is not a life-or-death fear, it's just your primitive brain on the loose. So flip your thinking into the gains and overpower any perceived losses.

How? Spend two minutes listing all the wonderful advantages you'll gain by achieving your goal. This will reconnect you with the gains and start to melt any loss-based fear. Like:

- If I spend less on eating out, I'll be able to afford an amazing holiday and have a serious adventure
- If I eat well, I will have more energy, feel lighter and my skin will be better
- Studying will expand my knowledge, train my brain and create a platform that will leverage my career

You may have noticed that these advantages look like a combination of the "whys" and healthy marshmallows that we looked at on days 15 and 16. That's because very often they are. Today's masterclass is designed to help you manage your fear of loss on a daily basis through your marshmallows, while you can also apply today's exercise whenever you need to overpower the fear of loss.

DAY 25 CHECK-IN

My goal is..
.

GOAL

ONE STEP AT A TIME

My daily marshmallows

1..

2..

3..

GOAL DATE

__/__/__

1. Morning power question

What can I do today to improve my motivational process?...
....

2. Evening check-in

Did I do my best to [insert goal step] today? What did I do?...
....

3. Streak checkbox

4. Score your positivity streams

#1 Sleep	#2 Movement	#3 Nutrition	#4 Connection	#5 Quiet time	#6 Clear thinking
1	1	1	1	1	1
2	2	2	2	2	2
3	3	3	3	3	3
4	4	4	4	4	4
5	5	5	5	5	5
6	6	6	6	6	6
7	7	7	7	7	7
8	8	8	8	8	8
9	9	9	9	9	9
10	10	10	10	10	10

DAY 26: STICK OR TWIST

Rich Roll had worked hard all his life as a lawyer, with the goal of supporting a happy, vibrant family. But something happened that was to change the way he viewed the world, which also changed his goals.

Aged 40, Rich climbed the stairs of his LA pad, and halfway up he had to stop because he was out of breath. In this moment he realized his financial goal was no longer making him happy. He was unhealthy and overweight. His epiphany on the stairs sparked the motivation to try something new. Something radical. He started running for the first time in years. Quickly he lost weight, got fit and felt alive again. And something inside him clicked – he knew he wanted to dedicate his life to running, health and fitness. So he made a radical goal shift. Rich quit his high-flying job and followed a new goal to compete in an ultra marathon.

You can imagine the conflict this created, as his original goal had been all about financial stability, and his new goal could mean a financial meltdown. As it happens, at one point Rich was down to his last few hundred dollars, before turning things around. Eventually he went on to run his ultra marathon, becoming one of the fittest men on the planet and a superhero in the world of wellbeing. His book *Finding Ultra* is a motivational gem, and his podcast is the best there is.

Rich is an extreme example of someone switching goals, but it's important to be aware that your outlook on life might change when you learn to master motivation and so might your goals. And there is nothing wrong with this. Because each goal you conquer will help you grow a little. So never be afraid to change, but make sure you do it in the right way to keep up your momentum.

What if you get this far only to realize you're shooting for the wrong star?

It's totally OK to change goals if you do it in the right way. There are no hard rules about when to pull the ripcord. But there are a few key things to consider when changing your one goal.

- Avoid hiding behind tired old excuses like "I don't have the motivation" because, as you have discovered, this is not true.

- As you learned yesterday, you might be scared. Sometimes your primitive brain takes over and demands that you get back in your comfort zone. So don't rush into changing your goal.
- Ask yourself, "Am I resisting this goal because I am not prepared to do the work required at this moment in my life?" There is nothing wrong with not wanting to do the work. What's critical is that you *acknowledge* you simply don't want to do the work or have the time to do the work at this stage of your life, rather than glossing over the truth with a veiled excuse such as "I am not good enough". Sometimes the effort required to achieve your goal can outweigh the upside, so it's a sensible choice to change.

Try this

This simple two-step exercise will either give you closure on a goal that was not serving you, or reconnect you with your current goal. Both outcomes are a win. You either move on with pride, or you re-align with your existing goal. Here goes:

Step 1 – Acknowledge the right reasons to move on
I acknowledge that I could achieve my goal to [insert goal], but I choose not to for the following reasons:

* ....

* ....

* ....

Example:
I acknowledge that I could achieve my goal to blog every day, but I choose not to for the following reasons:
* Having made the effort, I realize I don't enjoy this process enough to consistently show up and write
* It was taking too much time from other areas of my life which matter more to me
* I am pleased that I took action, but now I realize this goal is not as important to me as I once thought

Step 2 – Are you ready to move on?

Do you still want to change goals? If, during the exercise above, you discover fear is making you want to stop and actually you do want to stick with your current goal, then revisit your motivational plan and keep tweaking it until it works.

If you still want to move on, then fire up the goal stacker once more (see page 78) and select your next goal. Most importantly, make sure to then set up your plan and take action.

DAY 26 CHECK-IN

My goal is...

GOAL

TIME
A
AT
STEP
ONE

My daily marshmallows

1...

2...

3...

GOAL DATE

__/__/__

I. Morning power question

What can I do today to improve my motivational process?...

....

2. Evening check-in

Did I do my best to [insert goal step] today? What did I do?...

....

3. Streak checkbox ☐

4. Score your positivity streams

#I Sleep	#2 Movement	#3 Nutrition	#4 Connection	#5 Quiet time	#6 Clear thinking
I	I	I	I	I	I
2	2	2	2	2	2
3	3	3	3	3	3
4	4	4	4	4	4
5	5	5	5	5	5
6	6	6	6	6	6
7	7	7	7	7	7
8	8	8	8	8	8
9	9	9	9	9	9
10	10	10	10	10	10

DAY 27: CELEBRATE THE RIGHT WAY

Before I figured out how motivation works, I cannot tell you on how many occasions I celebrated a few weeks of being "good" and sticking to my goal plan, with a moment of being "bad". And it's not just me, it's all of us, as far as I can tell. Think about it: have you ever had a few days or weeks off alcohol and thought, I know, I will celebrate my perfectness with a beer or glass of wine?

This strange phenomenon can appear within any of our goals. We celebrate a week of salads with a cake-fest. Or the month of saving with a massive spend-up. If this is you, don't panic, we all do it and it's called moral licensing.

What do points make?

When you view your goal steps as being *good,* you create an imaginary points system in your brain. And what do points make? Prizes. And guess who is in charge of the scoring system? Your primitive brain, so the results are a fix. When you score enough *good* points, very often the prize is to trust your impulses or let your primitive brain decide how to celebrate, which often ends in you doing something bad.

Ravi Dhar, Management Professor at Yale, and Ayelet Fishbach, a professor at the Chicago Graduate School of Business, demonstrated how moral licensing influences the celebrations of dieters. When participants in their study were reminded of how good they had been in achieving weight loss and then offered a celebratory gift of an apple or a chocolate bar, a massive 85 per cent chose the naughty option over the apple. The influence of moral licensing was exposed when a subsequent group, who were not told how "good" they had been, selected the naughty option only 58 per cent of the time.

But it's not all bad. When you're prepared, you can sidestep moral licensing and celebrate in the right way that will keep up the momentum toward your goal.

Here are three ways to overcome those bad celebrations:

WE CELEBRATE A WEEK OF SALADS WITH A CAKE-FEST

THE "BAD" TREAT LOOKED LIKE A THREAT TO THEIR DREAMS AND NOT A TREAT AFTER ALL

Remember your "whys"

A combined effort from researchers at the University of Chicago and the Hong Kong University of Science and Technology shows us an almost magical way to stop our primitive brain from keeping score. Once again, the researchers used a good and bad celebratory food option to test the effects of moral licensing. First, one group of students were asked to remember a time when they had been "good" and had turned down temptation. Just thinking of these good points allowed moral licensing to flourish and a whopping 70 per cent of the students went on to indulge in the naughty option at the very next opportunity. But what happened next had an almost magical power to reverse the moral licensing and put our primitive brain back in its box. The next set of students were asked to remember why they had resisted temptation and the result was reversed, with 69 per cent avoiding the "bad" option.

Just remembering why had reconnected the students with their goal, so the "bad" treat looked like a threat to their dreams and not a treat after all. Also, the students were conscious that they had control to act in a way that was in keeping with their goal ambitions, which helped them make the right choice.

So today, reconnect with all those reasons why you set out on your goal adventure (see day 1). Be sure to add in any new reasons and write them down to make the exercise more powerful.

Mini celebrations

You have already heard from the genius behavioural scientist B J Fogg (see page 116) who recommended you have a mini celebration each time you perform a goal step, to help lock in the new habit. And, as you know, the name of the 28-day game is to push your goal steps into your subconscious as a habit or core value. So these mini celebrations can really help.

A mini fist pump will suffice, or can you say – in your head, or out loud if you are feeling brave – "You're awesome", or something similar that will inspire you or make you laugh. Experiment with what works for you, but please add this to your motivational plan. Mini celebrations will make a difference.

Stack up your 28-day celebrations in advance

Remember, if you find yourself having a nice conversation in your head about how you should celebrate, there is a high chance the points scorer, your primitive brain, will get to decide. And you will end up sabotaging your dreams. So the trick is to plan in advance so there is no conversation. You will know exactly how you are going to celebrate.

If you stick to the 28-day principle, you will need about 12 celebrations per year. Why not use this as an excuse to get organized in advance, so your whole year is punctuated with cool, fun celebratory things to do?

Take some time today to brainstorm as many celebrations as you can and line them up. Aim to have 12. In doing so you're pre-registering your intent to crush your goals for the next year. This is the mindset of a motivational maestro.

Also, knowing in advance how you will celebrate will help you stay focused, remove any moral licensing and unleash a bagload of positive emotions that will broaden your thinking to help you reach more goals.

As you will see, it does not take loads of effort and, once you have your list, lock the dates in and book the celebrations wherever possible. Stay focused in on your celebration throughout your 28 days. Keep your mind on this bonus prize, because it will motivate you. And finally it makes the year look really exciting.

To give you an idea, here is what my last rewards list looked like:

January: ski trip
February: sun break (have to get a bit of winter sun)
March: massage/spa day
April: permaculture course (bit geeky, but I love it)
May: hike
June: walk
July: holiday
August: Ireland trip to see mates and walk
September: theatre
October: dinner somewhere nice
November: winter sun trip
December: winter hike

DAY 27 CHECK-IN

My goal is...
.

GOAL

TIME

A

AT

STEP

ONE

My daily marshmallows

1...

2...

3...

GOAL DATE

__/ __/ __

1. Morning power question

What can I do today to improve my motivational process?...

....

2. Evening check-in

Did I do my best to [insert goal step] today? What did I do?...

....

3. Streak checkbox

4. Score your positivity streams

#1 Sleep	#2 Movement	#3 Nutrition	#4 Connection	#5 Quiet time	#6 Clear thinking
1	1	1	1	1	1
2	2	2	2	2	2
3	3	3	3	3	3
4	4	4	4	4	4
5	5	5	5	5	5
6	6	6	6	6	6
7	7	7	7	7	7
8	8	8	8	8	8
9	9	9	9	9	9
10	10	10	10	10	10

DAY 28: YOU DID IT!

You are now officially on your way to motivational mastery. I am super-proud of you. And thank you for sticking around long enough to learn all the techniques, ideas and skills. It takes a lot of courage to think differently and even more bravery to behave differently.

Hopefully you now realize that you always had plenty of motivation – it was just misdirected. You are not broken or weak-willed. You are a perfectly imperfect human who now has a motivational plan.

The last 28 days have been the start of your lifetime quest to master motivation and in doing so master your life. You now know that motivation is a skill you can learn and master, and you have just experienced some of the best motivational concepts, ideas and techniques that will last you a lifetime.

But there is still one day to go…

Exercise: own your insights

Today I want you to own all the insights you have uncovered from this book.

A great way to do this is to write them down. My dream is that you can walk away from this book and in six months or six years still carry these insights in your mind, so that if someone were to ask you, "What do you know about motivation?", you could amaze them with your practical knowledge, because you are still using these ideas on a daily basis to crush your goals.

So take some time to reflect, flick back through the book, list your best insights and commit them to memory. Carry these motivational gems at the forefront of your mind.

Before we wrap up the masterclass, I would love to know – what is the biggest hurdle you have overcome during the last 28 days? Once again, write this down somewhere if you can, to add some extra visceral power.

Then finally, take a few moments to look back and feel the confidence in your chest as you realize how far you have already come. And remember the time machine, because you're just warming up.

DAY 28 CHECK-IN

My goal is..

GOAL

My daily marshmallows

1...

2...

3...

GOAL DATE

__/__/__

1. Morning power question
What can I do today to improve my motivational process?...

....

2. Evening check-in
Did I do my best to [insert goal step] today? What did I do?..

....

3. Streak checkbox

4. Score your positivity streams

#1 Sleep	#2 Movement	#3 Nutrition	#4 Connection	#5 Quiet time	#6 Clear thinking
1	1	1	1	1	1
2	2	2	2	2	2
3	3	3	3	3	3
4	4	4	4	4	4
5	5	5	5	5	5
6	6	6	6	6	6
7	7	7	7	7	7
8	8	8	8	8	8
9	9	9	9	9	9
10	10	10	10	10	10

What you learned this week

Day 22 – Outsource motivation: outsourcing can work great, if you own it

Day 23 – Get your gut onside: give your microbiome the right foods to fuel your goals

Day 24 – A brush with death: let "memento mori" motivate you to enjoy every second of your day

Day 25 – Love the fear: your goals will scare you and this is a sign you are on the right path

Day 26 – Stick with the goal or change: you can change goals and keep your momentum

Day 27 – Celebrate the right way: celebrate your wins in a way that supports your goals

Day 28 – You did it: now you're on your way to motivational mastery

What Now? Complete the Motivational Loop

Congratulations on reaching the end of your first 28-day masterclass! But this is not the finish, this is just the start. Over the last four weeks you have completed one full loop of your motivational plan. You're still a beginner, but you now have the foundation to become a black belt.

How do you get there? By practising the skill of motivation over and over. In the same way you would need to keep lifting weights or painting to master your body or your art. Remember, motivation is a skill which needs to be practised daily. So let's have a look at where you are now:

Is your goal complete?

If so, now is the time to start the next one. Motivation is about momentum, so build on your hard work, fire up the goal stacker and kick-start your next most important goal. Get tactical. Could you improve one of your six streams of positivity scores first to give you more motivation for your subsequent goal?

Is your goal ongoing?

Give yourself a pat on the back – this is perfectly normal. Lots of goals take longer than 28 days. What you're trying to achieve after 28 days are the daily habits required to reach your goal, even if it's not your main focus.

For example, if your goal was to run a marathon in six months, then the aim of the masterclass was to help you install the habits required to continually show up and execute the daily steps until you complete your goal and run those 42km (26 miles).

Do you need more time?

If you want more time with a goal, stick with it. There are no wrongs or rights. Changing an ingrained habit like smoking might take longer than 28 days to push down into the core of your being. In my experience it takes closer to 90 days to transform your relationship with alcohol, so be brave enough to stay with any goals that are not yet running as a subconscious habit or core value.

Your life is a gigantic experiment. So test what works for you. If your previous goal starts to slip, pause the current one, go back to the one that's slipping and give it your love. When you're confident it's back on track and you have strong enough habits in place, unpause the next goal and move on.

Before you start your next goal, consider the following questions:

- Do you need more time with the current goal to push the daily steps into a subconscious habit or value?
- If you were to start a new goal, could you maintain the previous routines required to reach your last goal?
- If you did not think about the current goal, would you still show up tomorrow and execute the routines to maintain it?
- If your goal does not have a defined ending, such as eating Paleo, are the habits and core values in place to maintain this lifestyle change?
- And finally, do you want to move on to your next goal? If you're loving your current goal and learning to master motivation, feel free to stick with it for a bit longer.

One thing is for certain: you now have a plan that will work with any goal you choose. You will no longer be bamboozled by the blank page. You get to build on the momentum you have just created.

This is the beauty of owning your motivational plan. You can reuse all the learning for your next goal and the one after. Each goal helps you to improve your motivational plan, so the subsequent goal is easier to achieve. It's a virtuous circle of motivation. And as you are about to find out, this book is not really about motivation, it's about your life.

And for My Last Trick...

What is it you really want? What are all these motivational struggles for?

The brook beneath our goals and dreams is a desire to find happiness. Our quest for happiness is what drives us forward and fuels meaning and purpose. But happiness, like motivation, is largely misunderstood.

Happiness doesn't lie at the end of the goal rainbow. Happiness lies in the struggle, not the end result. But what you might not realize is that happiness is not just about those feel-good, positive emotions. Happiness or wellbeing is about so much more.

Let me explain. Twenty years ago, a chap called Martin Seligman was weeding his garden. Lost in thought, he was interrupted by his daughter. "Dad, Dad!" she cried. "Does E really equal MC squared?" (That's a joke. Not all clever people spawn mini geniuses. She actually said, "Dad, come and play, please come and play.")

Seligman snapped back, "No. Can't you see I'm busy?"

Through her tears his daughter replied, "You're a grouch."

"Grouch" was a one-word punch in the motivational stomach. Seligman knew his daughter was right. He was a grouch. In that moment he vowed to use science to help him uncover techniques that would lead to happiness and cure him of his grouchiness.

You see, Seligman was no ordinary grouch. He had just been appointed head of the American Psychological Society. This is the biggest job in psychology, and part of Seligman's tenure was to provide direction for psychology as a whole. Following his garden epiphany, Seligman decided to take psychology back to its roots.

Rather than just focusing on pathology and healing the sick, part of psychology's original mission was to nurture talent and find ways to improve the wellbeing of individuals and communities. Over the years the positive side of psychology had been forgotten. That was until 1998, when Seligman pioneered the positive psychology movement.

At the core of positive psychology are the PERMA elements of wellbeing or happiness: Positive emotion, Engagement, Relationships, Meaning and Accomplishment. Seligman and his researchers spent years reading the best science, while learning from the great thinkers and philosophers to help define wellbeing, as they like to call it. And they uncovered something very important: happiness is not just about positive emotions. It's a combination of all the PERMA elements.

Over the years, Seligman and a growing army of positive psychologists have applied science to consistently demonstrate that each of the PERMA elements has a positive effect on health and wellbeing, and can even help you live longer.

For many years I worked hard on the individual PERMA elements, but it was not until I mastered motivation that I discovered the final truth.

As it turns out, happiness is threaded into the motivational struggle to achieve your goals. You will find tons of positive emotions inside your healthy marshmallows. Those small wins in the moment and a sense of accomplishment flood your mind and body with feel-good emotions. Striving toward your goals often ignites a deep engagement or flow as your whole mind and body is immersed in the task. Time stops and you become like an athlete in the zone.

My favourite of all the PERMA elements – relationships – continually improve as you find your energy, make connection a priority and discover who you really are.

Finally, the six streams of positivity and your motivational plan merge to offer you a shot at the title – meaning and purpose, which completes the circle of happiness and a life well lived.

And if it holds that ultimately we all just want to be happy, then mastering your motivation should be your life's work. This is the true secret of this book. It's not really about motivation. It's about unlocking your most vibrant, happy life. Let's do this!

HAPPINESS DOESN'T LIE AT THE
END OF THE GOAL RAINBOW.
HAPPINESS LIES IN THE STRUGGLE,
NOT THE END RESULT

References

PART I

CHAPTER I

page 11 *In the 1960s...*

Mischel, Walter, *The Marshmallow Test: Understanding self-control and how to master it*. London: Transworld, 2015, p. 283

page 12 *Several years after the original marshmallows test...*

Mischel, W., Shoda, Y., and P. K. Peake, "The Nature of Adolescent Competencies Predicted by Preschool Delay of Gratification", *Journal of Personality and Social Psychology* 54, no. 4, 1988: pp. 687–99

Mischel, W., Shoda, Y., and M. L. Rodriguez, "Delay of Gratification in Children", *Science* 244, no. 4907, 1989: pp. 933–8

Shoda, Y., Mischel, W., and P. K. Peake, "Predicting Adolescent Cognitive and Social Competence from Preschool Delay of Gratification: Identifying diagnostic conditions", *Developmental Psychology* 26, no. 6, 1990, pp. 978–86

page 14 *Another brilliant scientist, the social psychologist Roy Baumeister...*

Baumeister, Roy F., and John Tierney, *Willpower: Why self-control is the secret to success*. New York: Penguin Press, 2011, p. 23

CHAPTER 2

page 35 *The science is almost overwhelming...*

Greger, Michael, and Gene Stone, *How Not To Die: Discover the foods scientifically proven to prevent and reverse disease*. London: MacMillan, 2015

CHAPTER 3

page 21 *A whopping 80 per cent of us...*

https://www.bristol.ac.uk/policybristol/news/2013/37.html

page 35 *Over 62 per cent of the UK population...*

Baker, Caril, *Obesity Statistics*. Briefing paper no. 3336, 6 August 2019. London: House of Commons Library

page 35 *One in two of us are unhappy in our jobs...*

https://www.lsbf.org.uk/media/2760986/final-lsbf-career-change-report.pdf

page 37 *Roy Baumeister of Florida State University...*

Baumeister, Roy F., and John Tierney, *Willpower: Why self-control is the secret to success*. London: Penguin Press, 2011, p. 23

Baumeister, R. F., Bratlavsky, E., Muraven, M., and D. M. Tice, "Ego Depletion: Is the active self a limited resource?" *Journal of Personality and Social Psychology* 74, 1998: pp. 1252–65

CHAPTER 4

page 41 *The second brain is the human, rational one…*
Harari, Yuval Noah, *Sapiens: A brief history of humankind.* London: Harvill Secker, 2014, p. 95

PART 2

CHAPTER 5

page 51 *One Year No Beer…*
https://www.oneyearnobeer.com/
page 52 *SMART goals are so boring…*
Doran, G. T., "There's a S.M.A.R.T. Way to Write Management's Goals and Objectives", *Management Review*, vol. 70, issue 11, 1981, pp. 35–6
page 56 *Some ingenious research from Sophie Leroy…*
Leroy, S., "Why is it so hard to do my work? The challenge of attention residue when switching between work tasks", *Organizational Behavior and Human Decision Processes*, vol. 109, issue 2, July 2009, pp. 168-81
page 56 *American computer scientist Cal Newport…*
Newport, Cal., *Deep Work: Rules for focused success in a distracted world.* London: Piatkus, 2016

CHAPTER 6

page 62 *A study of New Zealand drivers…*
Williamson, A. M., and A. M. Feyer, "Moderate Sleep Deprivation Produces Impairments in Cognitive and Motor Performance Equivalent to Legally Prescribed Levels of Alcohol Intoxication", *Journal of Occupational and Environmental Medicine*, vol. 57, issue 10, October 2000, pp. 649–55
page 62 *Nick Littlehales is the author…*
Littlehales, Nick, *Sleep: The myth of 8 hours, the power of naps…and the new plan to recharge your body and mind.* London: Penguin, 2016, p. 180
page 62 *Research from Harvard Medical School…*
https://hms.harvard.edu/sites/default/files/assets/Sites/Longwood_Seminars/Sleep_3_19_13.pdf
page 65 *Experts call this movement NEAT…*
Levine, J., "Nonexercise Activity Thermogenesis (NEAT): environment and biology", *American Journal of Physiology-Endocrinology and Metabolism*, vol. 288(1), E285, January 2005
page 70 *The last survey, in 2014…*
McPherson, M., *et al.*, "Social Isolation in America: Changes in core discussion networks over two decades", *American Sociological Review* 71, 2006: pp. 353–75
page 70 *Australian author Bronnie Ware sums up the power of connection…*
Ware, Bronnie, *The Top Five Regrets of the Dying: A life transformed by the dearly departing.* London: Hay House, 2012

page 72 *A few years ago I invited Dr Itai Ivtzan…*

Ivtzan, Itai, *Awareness Is Freedom: The adventure of psychology and spirituality*. Alresford, Hants: Changemakers Books, 2015

page 74 *Research shows that alcohol destroys the deep, restorative phase of sleep…*

Ebrahim, I., Shapiro, C., Williams, A., and P. Fenwick, "Alcohol and Sleep I: Effects on normal sleep", *Alcohol. Clin. Exp. Res.* vol. 37, issue 4, April 2013, pp. 539–49

CHAPTER 7

page 85 *Let's first learn how to create a habit…*

Duhigg, Charles, *The Power of Habit: Why we do what we do and how to change*. London: Random House, 2013

page 87 *What can sport teach us about motivation?*

https://www.telegraph.co.uk/world-cup/2018/07/04/england-conquered-penalty-shootout-hoodo-review-past-failures/

page 88 *Let me introduce Harry Harlow…*

Harlow, Harry F., Harlow, Margaret Kuenne, and Donald R. Meyer, "Learning Motivated by a Manipulation Drive", *Journal of Experimental Psychology* 40, 1950, p. 231

page 89 *Like Newton's apple, this was a reality-shifting discovery…*

Pink, Daniel H., *Drive: The surprising truth about what motivates us*. Edinburgh: Canongate, 2018

page 90 *Building on what Harlow discovered back in 1950…*

Ryan, Richard M., and Edward L. Deci, *Self-Determination Theory: Basic psychological needs in motivation, development, and wellness*. New York: Guilford Press, 2017

Ryan, R. M., and E. L. Deci, "Self-Determination Theory and the Facilitation of Intrinsic Motivation, Social Development, and Well-Being", *American Psychologist* 55, 2000, pp. 68–78

CHAPTER 8

page 94 *As psychologist Douglas Lisle explains…*

Lisle, Douglas J., and Alan Goldhamer, *The Pleasure Trap: Mastering the hidden force that undermines health and happiness*. Summertown, TN: Book Publishing Company, 2003, p. 8

page 95 *When we stopped hunting and gathering…*

Harari, Yuval Noah, *Sapiens: A brief history of humankind*. London: Harvill Secker, 2014, p. 46

PART 3

DAY 1

page 112 *Look at Jerry Seinfeld…*

https://lifehacker.com/jerry-seinfelds-productivity-secret-281626

page 112 *The researchers compared 138 studies…*

Harkin, B., Webb, T. L., Chang, B. P. I. *et al.*, "Does Monitoring Goal

Progress Promote Goal Attainment? A meta-analysis of the experimental evidence", *Psychological Bulletin*, 142 (2), 2016, pp. 198–229

DAY 2

page 115 *Charles Duhigg, whom we met...*
Duhigg, Charles, *The Power of Habit: Why we do what we do and how to change*. London: Random House, 2013
page 116 *B J Fogg is the director...*
https://www.tinyhabits.com/

DAY 3

page 119 *During a One Year No Beer podcast I did with Rosamund Dean...*
https://www.oneyearnobeer.com/finding-clarity-oynb-podcast-030/
page 119 *Some brilliant research from...*
Ericsson, Anders, and Robert Pool, *Peak: How all of us can achieve extraordinary things*. London: Vintage, 2017
page 119 *Bill Gates offered more timely wisdom...*
Read more at https://www.brainyquote.com/quotes/bill_gates_404193

DAY 4

page 122 *So I gave up. Until two years later...*
Elrod, Hal, *The Miracle Morning: The 6 Habits That Will Transform Your Life Before 8am* (p. 103), John Murray Press: Kindle Edition
page 123 *Remember what the Roman philosopher Seneca said...*
Seneca, *On the Shortness of Life*. London: Penguin Great Ideas, 2004

DAY 6

page 130 *Jim Rohn, a motivational guru...*
https://www.goodreads.com/quotes/1798-you-are-the-average-of-the-five-people-you-spend
page 130 *Network researcher Nicholas Christakis...*
Christakis, Nicholas, and James Fowler, *Connected: The amazing power of social networks and how they shape our lives*. London: Harper Press, 2011
page 131 *Back in the days when we roamed the savannah...*
Wright, Robert, *The Moral Animal: Evolutionary psychology and everyday life*. London: Abacus, 1996
page 134 *Here's my dream boat crew for my goal of writing this book...*
Newport, Cal, *Deep Work: Rules for focused success in a distracted world*. London: Piatkus, 2016
Goggins, David, *Can't Hurt Me: Master your mind and defy the odds*. Austin, TX: Lioncrest Publishing, 2018
Holiday, Ryan, *Perennial Seller: The art of making and marketing work that lasts*. London: Profile, 2017

DAY 8

page 141 *Why kindness works...*

Izadi, Shahroo, *The Kindness Method: Changing habits for good*. London: Bluebird, 2018

page 141 *Some brilliant research from the Carleton University in Ottawa...*
Wohl, M. J. A., Pychyl, T. A., and S. H. Bennett, "I Forgive Myself, Now I Can Study: How self-forgiveness for procrastinating can reduce future procrastination", *Personality and Individual Differences* 48, 2010, pp. 803–8

DAY 10

page 151 *Cornelius Celsus wrote an encyclopedia...*
Celsus C. A. *De Medicina* (On Medicine), Book VII. (*c.* AD30) Loeb Classical Library Edition, 1935

page 151 *This new wave of nature-based science confirmed...*
Selhub, E., and Logan, A., *Your Brain On Nature*. Toronto: Collins, 2014

page 152 *I was astounded to discover that 47 per cent of London is green space...*
https://www.independent.co.uk/environment/47-per-cent-of-london-is-green-space-is-it-time-for-our-capital-to-become-a-national-park-9756470.html

page 152 *Brain imaging techniques have revealed that even pictures of nature...*
Kim, H., et al., "Human brain activation in response to visual stimulation and rural urban scenery pictures: A functional magnetic resonance imaging study", *Sci Total Environ* 2010: 48:2600–7

page 152 *House plants are like mini-motivators...*
Yamane, K., *et al*, "Effects of interior horticultural activities with potted plants on human physiological and emotional status", *Acta Hortic* 2004; 639:37–43

page 152 *Research has shown that participants who took...*
Roe, J., and Aspinall, P., "The restorative benefits of walking in urban and rural settings in adults with good and poor mental health", *Health Place* 2011; 17:103–13

DAY 11

page 155 *Dr Steve Peters, the genius psychiatrist behind many athletes...*
Peters, Steve, *The Chimp Paradox: The mind management programme to help you achieve success, confidence and happiness*. London: Vermilion, 2012

DAY 12

page 159 *In his book* Changing for Good...
Prochaska, James O., *et al.*, *Changing for Good: A revolutionary six-stage program for overcoming bad habits and moving your life positively forward*. New York: HarperCollins, 2006, p. 22

page 159 *He created a scientific model of how people change...*
Diclemente, C. C., and J. O. Prochaska, "Toward a Comprehensive, Transtheoretical Model of Change: Stages of change and addictive behaviours", in Miller, W. R., and N. Heather, ed., *Treating Addictive Behaviors*, second edition, New York: Plenum Press, 1998, pp. 3–24

page 159 *You see, Prochaska's model revealed a great secret...*

DiClemente, C. C., Prochaska, J. O., Fairhurst, S. K., Velicer, W. F., Velasquez, M. M., and J. S. Rossi. "The Process of Smoking Cessation: An analysis of pre-contemplation, contemplation, and preparation stages of change", *Journal of Consulting and Clinical Psychology*, 59(2), 1991, pp. 295–304

page 160 *Some brilliant research from Strava...*
https://www.independent.co.uk/life-style/quitters-day-new-years-resolutions-give-up-fail-today-a8155386.html

DAY 13

page 163 *The Ukatak is held in the middle of the Canadian winter...*
De Sena, Joe, *Spartan Up! A take-no-prisoners guide to overcoming obstacles and peak performance in life.* London: Simon & Schuster, 2014

page 164 *What do tribes mean for motivation?*
Griskevicius, V., J. M. Tybur, and B. Van den Bergh, "Going Green to Be Seen: Status, reputation, and conspicuous conservation", *Journal of Personality and Social Psychology* 98, 2010, pp. 392–404

page 164 *Some great research from Jessica Nolon...*
Nolan, J. M., P. W. Schultz, R. B. Cialdini, N. J. Goldstein, and V. Griskevicius. "Normative Social Influence Is Under-detected." *Personality and Social Psychology Bulletin* 34 (2008): 913–23

page 164 *If you want to get fit...*
https://www.parkrun.org.uk/

page 164 *If you have a goal of public speaking...*
https://www.toastmasters.org/

DAY 14

page 166 *My hero in the addiction space...*
Peele, Stanton, *Recover!: Stop thinking like an addict and reclaim your life with the PERFECT program.* Boston, MA: Da Capo Lifelong Books, 2014, p. 15

page 166 *And don't forget, as Nicholas Christakis shows us...*
Rosenquist, J. N., Murabito, J., Fowler, H. J., and N. A. Christakis, "The Spread of Alcohol Consumption Behavior in a Large Social Network", *Annals of Internal Medicine* 152, 2010, pp. 426–33

DAY 15

page 171 *One bright Sunday November morning, Ross Edgley emerged...*
https://www.redbull.com/gb-en/projects/great-british-swim

DAY 17

page 180 *The guru of state change, Tony Robbins...*
Robbins, Tony, *Awaken the Giant Within: How to take immediate control of your mental, emotional, physical and financial life.* London: Simon & Schuster, 1992, revised edition 2001, p. 184

page 181 *In her book* Maximum Willpower...
McGonigal, Kelly, *Maximum Willpower: How to master the new science of self-control.* London: Pan Macmillan, 2012

DAY 18

page 186 *In one of the most motivational books you will ever read...*
Goggins, David, *Can't Hurt Me: Master your mind and defy the odds.*
Austin, TX: Lioncrest Publishing, 2018

DAY 19

page 188 *When I first met Catherine Gray...*
Gray, Catherine, *The Unexpected Joy of Being Sober: Discovering a happy, healthy, wealthy alcohol-free life.* London: Aster, 2017
page 188 *Barbara Fredrickson is Professor of Psychology...*
Fredrickson, Barbara, *Positivity: Groundbreaking research to release your inner optimist and thrive.* New York: Crown Publishers, 2009
page 188 *Fredrickson developed the "broaden and build" theory...*
Fredrickson, Barbara L., "The Role of Positive Emotions in Positive Psychology: The broaden-and-build theory of positive emotions", *American Psychologist,* vol. 56(3), March 2001, pp. 218–226
page 190 *The positive bonuses don't end there...*
Danner, Deborah D. *et al.* "Positive emotions in early life and longevity: findings from the nun study." *Journal of personality and social psychology* 80 5 (2001): 804-13

DAY 20

page 192 *Ryan and Deci, the researchers who created self-determination theory...*
Ryan, Richard M., and Edward L. Deci, *Self-Determination Theory: Basic psychological needs in motivation, development, and wellness.* New York: Guilford Press, 2017
page 192 *Carol Dweck is the queen of mindset...*
Dweck, Carol S., *Mindset: Changing the way you think to fulfil your potential.* New York: Random House, 2006; updated edition London: Robinson, 2017
page 193 *Robert Greene, author of* Mastery...
Greene, Robert, *Mastery.* New York: Viking, 2012

DAY 21

page 197 *About 2,000 years ago, the great Stoic philosopher Epictetus...*
Epictetus, *Enchiridion.* Mineola, NY: Dover Thrift Editions, 2004
page 197 *It was another quote from Epictetus...*
Evans, Jules, *Philosophy for Life and Other Dangerous Situations.* London: Rider, 2012

DAY 23

page 206 *It's because we have trillions of microbes in our gut...*
Gershon, Michael D., *The Second Brain: A groundbreaking new understanding of nervous disorders of the stomach and intestine.* New York: HarperColllins, 1998
page 208 *Scientist Scott Anderson sums up...*
Anderson, Scott C., *et al., The Psychobiotic Revolution.* Washington, DC: *National Geographic,* 2017, p. 15

page 208 *My great mate Dr Alan Desmond...*
@devongutdoctor on Instagram

DAY 24
page 212 *Then I read* The Daily Stoic...
Holiday, Ryan, and Stephen Hanselman, *The Daily Stoic: 366 meditations on wisdom, perseverance, and the art of living.* London: Profile Books, 2016

DAY 25
page 216 *"The cave you most fear to enter holds the treasure you seek..."*
Campbell, Joseph, *The Hero with a Thousand Faces.* Novato, CA: New World Library, 2012
page 216 *Or as Susan Jeffers urges...*
Jeffers, Susan, *Feel the Fear and Do It Anyway: How to turn your fear and indecision into confidence and action.* London: Vermilion, 2017

DAY 26
page 220 Rich Roll had worked hard all his life as a lawyer...
Roll, Rich, *Finding Ultra: Rejecting middle age, becoming one of the world's fittest men, and discovering myself.* New York: Three Rivers Press, 2012, pp. 2–3

DAY 27
page 224 *Ravi Dhar, Management Professor at Yale...*
Fishbach, A., and R. Dhar, "Goals as Excuses or Guides: The liberating effect of perceived goal progress on choice", *Journal of Consumer Research* 32, 2005: pp. 370–7
page 227 *A combined effort from researchers*
Mukhopadhyay, A., Sengupta, J., and S. Ramanathan, "Recalling Past Temptations: An information-processing perspective on the dynamics of self-control", *Journal of Consumer Research* 35, 2008: pp. 586–99

WHAT NOW? COMPLETE THE MOTIVATIONAL LOOP
page 235 *Twenty years ago, a chap called Martin Seligman...*
Seligman, Martin, *Flourish: A new understanding of happiness and well-being – and how to achieve them.* London: Nicholas Brealey Publishing, 2011, pp. 163–4

Index

Acknowledgements

A book on motivation requires its very own dream boat and my crew have all been a major influence on forming these ideas into this book.

Firstly, I would like to thank my wonderful wife Tara, my beautiful girls Molly and Ruby and my parents Kath and Jim, who will always be my greatest motivators.

Also, my deepest thanks to the OneYearNoBeer team, especially Ruari Fairbairns for allowing me the time and the space to write the book. To those friends, family and key people who helped me shape the structure and content within the book including Lenny McAuliffe, Colm Carrol, Mark Reeve, Russell Quirk, Bradley Tilson, Mark Kelly, Jamie Spicer, Brendan Aspinall, Andrew Stevenson (Strac), Phil Ramage, Rae Gilder Cooke, Rob Ramage, Richard Taggart and the fabulous Kate Faithfull-Williams.

It would be remiss of me not to mention some of the wonderful scientists whose shoulders I have climbed upon, including Walter Mischel, Richard Ryan, Edward Deci, Roy Baumeister, Harry Harlow and James Prochaska. And, of course, those motivational characters whose stories I have shared, including Joe De Sena, Rich Roll, David Goggins, Gary Allen, Fiona Roche, Jerry Lyons, Troy Doyle, Shahroo Izadi, Catherine Gray, Itai Ivtzan and Ross Edgely.

I must also thank my fantastic book agent Jane Graham-Maw for her support and her ability to connect the dots to make this book happen. And, finally, my team at Octopus: the wonderful Kate Adams who totally got behind the concept of the book and Polly Poulter for her gentle, but very persuasive, prompts to work the book into its best possible shape.

Thank you one and all.

About the Author

Andy Ramage is co-founder of OneYearNoBeer, an author, entrepreneur and behavioural change expert.

Andy Ramage is a former professional athlete who, after injury, cut short his career and went on to co-create two multimillion-dollar city brokerages.

After transforming his life and business due to a provocative break from alcohol, Andy was inspired to co-found the world-leading behavioural change platform OneYearNoBeer.com, which is a 28-, 90- or 365-day alcohol-free challenge that has inspired more than 100,000 people to transform their relationship with alcohol and power up their lives.

Andy holds a masters degree in coaching psychology and positive psychology and will start his PhD in 2020.

Andy's unique background, education and experience make him one of the world's leading behavioural change experts. He regularly speaks about behavioural change, peak performance and motivation. *Let's Do This* is his first book.

Website: www.andyramage.com
LinkedIn: https://www.linkedin.com/in/andyramage/
Facebook @MostlyPlantsAndWater
Instagram: @_andyramage